THE NEW MIDWEST

A Guide to Contemporary Fiction of the Great Lakes, Great Plains, and Rust Belt

Mark Athitakis

First edition 2016

ISBN: 978-0-9977742-8-3

Belt Publishing
1667 E. 40th Street #1G1
Cleveland, Ohio 44120
www.beltmag.com

Book design by Meredith Pangrace
Cover by David Wilson

Table of Contents

INTRODUCTION:

The Past and Present of the Fiction of the Midwest (Wherever That Is)

A few years ago I noticed something about my favorite works of contemporary fiction set in the Midwest: they were all set in the past. Jeffrey Eugenides' *Middlesex* (2002) is a sweeping tale that mostly takes place in 1960s Detroit. Marilynne Robinson's Iowa-set novels)—*Gilead* (2004), *Home* (2008), and *Lila* (2014)—explore the state in the middle of the twentieth century. Ward Just's *An Unfinished Season* (2004) spotlights upper-class journalists and lower-class laborers in 1950s Chicago. Celeste Ng's *Everything I Never Told You* (2014) is set in 1970s Ohio. Chris Ware's *Jimmy Corrigan: The Smartest Kid on Earth* (2000) is thick with flashbacks to Chicago's 1893 Columbian Exposition—an event that, thanks to Erik Larson's 2003 blockbuster historical true-crime tale, *The Devil in the White City*, seems to be the only Midwestern story people find interesting en masse besides cop and hospital dramas. And on and on.

This struck me as a problem. Why were writers considering the Midwest as a place where things *happened*, but no longer did? Earlier generations of writers didn't behave this way. The canonical Midwest writers—Willa Cather, Theodore Dreiser, Saul Bellow, Ernest Hemingway, Richard Wright—all wrote about Illinois,

Michigan, Nebraska, and Ohio in their moment, using their fiction for journalistic, way-we-live-now purposes at a transformative moment for the region. Through the first half of the twentieth century and much of the postwar period, the American economy shifted from agricultural to urban, and the migration of blacks from the South and immigrants from Europe made the Midwest an industrial powerhouse, and a rich breeding ground for social conflict to boot. Sinclair Lewis satirized that moment; Wright condemned the racism that accompanied it; Bellow celebrated transcending it. But as the twenty-first century approached—and as the Midwest lived in a new moment, one when its manufacturing might continued a steady decline that began in the 1970s and 1980s—some of the most prominent novelists and short-story writers weren't keeping up. Indeed, they seemed to gaze mostly backward at the region. In 1966, Robert Coover, a writer as eager as any postwar American novelist to challenge literary orthodoxy, published *The Origin of the Brunists,* an epic novel about an Illinois mine explosion hardly a decade past. In 2014, he delivered an epic sequel about what happened . . . five days later.

Not every Midwestern writer is caught in this time warp. Aleksandar Hemon writes about contemporary Chicago with a seriocomic grace. Gillian Flynn isn't just a master of page-turning plot twists, but a savvy thinker about the intersection of the Midwest and South in today's Missouri bootheel. Bonnie Jo Campbell and Stewart O'Nan have written sharp fiction about middle-class survivors in present-day Michigan and Pennsylvania. Jonathan Franzen is much-mocked for (among many, many other things) being forever conflicted about whether Midwestern values are a boon or bane, but he considers those values as they're being lived now. In the past decade or so, stories about the economic decline of the Rust Belt and Detroit have stoked novels like Philipp Meyer's *American Rust* (2009) and Angela Flournoy's *The Turner House* (2015).

Even those books, though, are often concerned with the past—that is, with what's been lost since the factories closed, after the verities of "Midwestern values" have eroded, once the promises of the region as one that welcomed immigrants and provided stability for blacks and Hispanics has crumbled. If they're not nostalgic for the past, they often lament what's been lost in the present.

But if today's Midwestern writers aren't on top of the news the way their precursors were, they aren't engaging in empty nostalgia either. Something more dialectical is going on: just as the books set in the present day are reckoning with the past, the books set in the past are also arguing with the present. Midwestern fiction today is a living manifestation of the tension between the region's old idealism and present-day reality. Robinson, Eugenides, Ng, and Just—and Jayne Anne Phillips and many more we'll get to—have used their novels to voice themes about race, sexuality, work, faith and more that they wouldn't have had the freedom to in the time when their books are set. That's a risky strategy that doesn't always make for persuasive fiction: implanting contemporary values upon the stories of the past is a tricky business if realism is your game. But I think Midwestern fiction is stronger for the number of writers who've risen to the task. The better writers on that front, such as Flynn, Ware, and Dinaw Mengestu, exploit the surfaces of the homey Midwest tale to smuggle in a more provocative or contemporary perspective. Contemporary American fiction is often dismissed as dealing in safe and gentle domestic family dramas set in white and upper-middle-class milieus. That's not what's happening in these books, though.

So why do we assume it does? Why does that reflex to see the Midwest as narrow and retrograde kick in so readily, years after the region has transformed from what it used to be?

One answer, in the form of a true story about the Midwest and baseball:

October 26, 2005. The Chicago White Sox are facing the Houston Astros in Game Four of the World Series, poised to win their first championship in eighty-eight years. At the bottom of the ninth inning, with the Sox one out away from a 1-0 victory and series sweep, Fox's live coverage in Houston cuts for a moment to Chicago and Jimbo's, a South Side sports bar full of cheering, boozy Sox fans. Amid the revelry, broadcaster Joe Buck solemnly puts the approaching victory into context.

"What does this mean to the South Side?" he asks, then offers a rough demographic sketch of the area. "A collection of neighborhoods like Beverly, Mount Greenwood, Hyde Park, Back-of-the-Yards, Canaryville, Bridgeport. Irish neighborhoods, Italian neighborhoods. Polish, Lithuanian. Firemen, policemen, school teachers, stockyard workers."

Stockyard workers.

Those two words say a lot — more than Buck likely intended. Like the Sox's championship drought, Buck's read on the city was a few decades out of date as well. As the Chicago journalist Alex Kotlowitz bemusedly noted in *Fast Company* after tuning in to the game, the last stockyard in the city closed in 1971. There was no reason why facts should get in the way of a good story on the verge of the White Sox's triumph, though; whether Buck studied his history or not, he was embracing a mythology that has long been connected the South Side — and to an extent, the greater Midwest. It's a romantic vision of a singularly hardworking place that welcomes floods of European immigrants and prides itself on the hard labor of construction, manufacturing, and meatpacking. If nobody can recite Carl Sandberg's 1914 poem "Chicago" anymore, they at least know it's the one that calls it the "City of the Big Shoulders" and the "stacker of wheat" and "Hog Butcher for the World." That's the myth: masculine, vibrant, busy.

It's a myth so powerful that we routinely neglect the lines in the same poem that undercut it. "Big Shoulders" and "Hog Butcher" have become such celebrated taglines for the city that you'd think the poem was an ode to the place. But it's more correct to say that "Chicago" is a kind of apology for the city: its encomiums are laced with observations about how "wicked," "crooked," and "brutal" the city is. Upton Sinclair struggled to deliver a similar critique of the city and stockyards in 1906, when his novel *The Jungle* was published. It's a memorable portrait of the degradations of the stockyards and their workers, rife with ghastly scenes of disease, poverty, and abusive labor practices. And it had an impact—it helped improve meat inspection and stoke the creation of what is now the Food and Drug Administration. But Sinclair had bigger ambitions for the book: he hoped to expose larger civic corrosion in Chicago and promote a socialist society that might correct it. So while the novel was a success, he only saw his ambition falling short. Chicago got credit for improving its meat, but its institutions had the same old case of botulism they always had. "I aimed at the public's heart," Sinclair once said, "and by accident hit its stomach."

So Joe Buck's praise of the stockyard workers was revealing on a couple of levels—not only was he romanticizing an industry that was notoriously dirty and corrupt, he was romanticizing one so closely tied to the city's fabric that its *decades-long* nonexistence in October 2005 hardly mattered. Buck was perpetuating a narrative of the Midwest as a place of earnest, big-shouldered, hardworking, churchy people. They may be wise to trouble—civic corruption, racial tensions—but the job of the good Midwesterner, the story goes, is to be untroubled and uncomplicated by it, to work through it. (Notably, Buck's vision of the South Side is constructed exclusively of white ethnics. No blacks in Bronzeville. No Latinos in Pilsen.)

Through much of the twentieth century, novelists writing about the Midwest have helped shore up this narrative, be it via realism or satire. It's in Saul Bellow's game Chicagoan Augie March, proudly announcing from the start of *The Adventures of Augie March* (1953) that he went at things freestyle, using the city as a launchpad for a host of ambitions; in Ernest Hemingway's young men discovering their masculinity in Michigan's Upper Peninsula; in Willa Cather's heartland settlers; in Sinclair Lewis's mockable conformists. In 1925, F. Scott Fitzgerald, a St. Paul, Minnesota, expat, published *The Great Gatsby*, a novel that thrust American literature into the Jazz Age and gave it a brisk, supple, unmistakably East Coast style. That same year, Theodore Dreiser delivered *An American Tragedy*, a hefty novel about guilt and doomed love in the Midwest. *Gatsby* was a study in flapper ambition and glamour and hubris, but *An American Tragedy* was formed out of more old-fashioned stuff, the values of work and love— and swift justice when the rules for both aren't adhered to.

This instinct to elevate some stories as "Midwestern" and diminish others has a long history, and it's one that endures. For proof, consider what happened in early 2016, when the website *Vox* set certain corners of the internet afire by asking users to identify which states are part of the Midwest. Is Nebraska part of the Midwest or the Great Plains? Is Cincinnati's culture more Midwestern or Southern? Why isn't Buffalo, a city with a long industrial history and that abuts one of the Great Lakes, not usually considered part of the Midwest? Within a day of the *Vox* article's publication, more than 34,000 people weighed in with their choices.

The strongest consensus about which state defined the Midwest was Iowa—a fact that provides a window into the factors that go into calling a place "Midwestern." In a 1998 essay titled "The Heartland's Role in US Culture: It's 'Main Street,'" University of Kansas professor James R. Shortridge writes that the term first came into use in the late 1800s in reference to Kansas and Nebraska—"Midwest" states in comparison to Minnesota and the

Dakotas, which were then the "Northwest." At the time, "Midwest" also spoke to a particular rural character: "People there were seen as self-reliant and independent, kind, open, and thrifty," Shortridge writes. "They were pragmatic and industrious, and they took pride in their work; yet they were also idealistic, moral, and humble."

Over time, cities complicated this optimistic, values-soaked vision, but Shortridge argues that culturally, the region never acquired a sophisticated reputation to match, certainly not the way the East Coast cities did. The Midwest was persistently rural—or, if not rural, indelibly marked by rural values. A perfect target for Sinclair Lewis, a perfect setting for Laura Ingalls Wilder—and perfect, in turn, for decades of nostalgic pining for a Midwest that never really existed. As racial tensions consumed cities like Chicago and Detroit and the eastern portions of the region endured economic collapse in the 1970s, Shortridge writes, "the public's response was to rework its collective cognitive map of Midwestern location. Ohio and Michigan were now partially excluded, and the regional core shifted to the Great Plains states." Detroit and Cleveland were now the Rust Belt; to preserve its utopian gleam, the "Midwest" picked up sticks and moved to Iowa.

The pattern is clear: the borders of the Midwest morph over time to define it as homey, religious, self-reliant, and white as possible. And the collective conception of Midwestern fiction has persistently matched those borders.

This book is an exploration of that mythology through recent fiction that's challenged it. Looking at a few dozen novels and story collections from the past three decades (and a few pertinent examples from further back), *The New Midwest* explores how writers have reconsidered the long-rutted narrative pathways that have defined the region. Hard work is not necessarily redemptive. Love isn't always submission. Nor is churchgoing. Detroit is neither a gleaming tribute to America's industrial might, nor a symbol of the country's ruination. Immigrants aren't universally noble, hardscrabble souls. It is, in short, a more complicated and questioning setting than it's been given credit for.

In this book, we'll keep the Midwest around the Great Lakes; we'll linger in the cities, we'll look at race. And when we do that, contemporary novels set in the Midwest become more vibrant reassertions of the complexity of the region. Angela Flournoy and Jeffrey Eugenides have delivered fierce counternarratives of the familiar Detroit industrial story. Aleksandar Hemon, Alaa Al Aswany, and Chris Ware have done the same for Chicago. Marilynne Robinson, whose name has become a shorthand for faithful, intellectual, good-hearted Iowa-ness, has in truth used her novels as spikier studies of the state's checkered past on race and religion. (Though as we'll see, it can be hard to find a critic to acknowledge it amid the rhetorical brush about her Midwestern integrity and suchlike.) Each of these writers acknowledges the optimistic pull of the cliché of Midwestern values, but also recognizes the economic damage, the racism and violence that are equally, if not more, defining.

I mean, if you were looking for an example of this hard-working, values-driven Midwest today, filled with honorable policemen, schoolteachers, stockyard workers, and such, where would you go? Perhaps you'd grab some inspiration from Joe Buck and head to Chicago's South Side and grab a beer at Jimbo's, that symbol of white-ethnic indomitability? Tough luck: it closed a year after the Sox won the Series. It had trouble making the rent.

M y goal in this book isn't to reshuffle the canon, ejecting old writers, inserting new ones, and rejiggering reputations. I admire Bellow and Cather and Wright and Hemingway and Nelson Algren and Sinclair Lewis— and even Upton Sinclair, a little. Many of them delivered the inspirational, transformative reading experiences I craved growing up in the Chicago suburbs, as it became clearer to me that I was living in a region with a particular history and sensibility. I just don't think that they any longer *exclusively* define the essence of Midwestern literature. Or, to put it a little more precisely, they no longer represent the core of what's relevant to a conversation about the Midwest.

This book is designed partly as a survey—a look at some of the most prominent and/or interesting novels and short story collections that take on the Midwest in unique ways. It's also a set of recommendations—though I don't love every book I discuss here equally, I believe they will reward your time spent reading and thinking about them. And this book is also an argument about how to think about the fiction of the Midwest. I look at these books through some common themes and connections—I believe that Marilynne Robinson and David Foster Wallace become more interesting when you look at them together as religious writers rather than as Iowa and Illinois writers. I think looking at faith, urbanity, race, family, and outsiderdom is a lot more interesting than lists of "best books" from particular states and regions. And I recognize the fluidity of the definition of the "Midwest." My selections generally stick close to the Mississippi River and the Great Lakes region. Chicago, yes, Cincinnati, no; Indiana and Ohio, but less so the Dakotas. But I can't neglect those borderlands entirely, and as we'll see, those places on the bubble are interesting in their own right.

Does this mean I've missed some important writers, perhaps even your favorite Midwest writer? Probably. I address some prominent writers bypassed in the main book at the end, in "What About…?" But a few gaps don't concern me overly much. If I've done my job, I've started a discussion, not settled it. People have passionate ideas not only about what the Midwest is, but what books best represent it. The main lesson is that the Midwest is a richer, more contrarian, more surprising place than the one we're encouraged to carry in our heads.

THE LATEST MIGRANTS

"A stranger comes to town" is the oldest story in the book, and in Midwestern fiction that story has tended to play out in two ways: immigrant and pioneer stories like Willa Cather's *My Ántonia* (1918) and Upton Sinclair's *The Jungle,* or Great Migration stories like *Native Son* (1940). The fates of the characters in those novels are radically different, but at heart they're effectively assimilation novels: the prevailing question is, *How do I become an American*? How do you make sense of the folkways that mark the country, from work to race, and successfully navigate them? This can play out in tragedy, as in *Native Son*, or as a conqueror's tale, as in *The Adventures of Augie March*. But the underlying assumption is that there is an underlying core of American-ness worth aspiring to.

In a time when the plains at the Midwest's far western edge were ample and open for homesteading, and when the city was a manufacturing hub that could support a quick rise up the ladder (or at least magnetized people who believed it could), the message in such novels felt right and timely. But when upward mobility is in doubt, when there is no one kind of American status to assimilate into, and there is less coherence to the region, what story do we tell now? The prevailing question today is now slightly different: *How do I become myself in this place?*

If a single work began highlighting this question, it's **Stuart Dybek**'s second story collection, *The Coast of Chicago* (1990). Dybek's gentler musings on Chopin and baseball replaced melodrama and steely prose about stockyards and empire builders. His sensibility was at once streetwise and omniscient, hyperaware of the forces that were affecting his imagined lower- and middle-class residents, mostly Poles, and also filled with highly individualized portraits of characters who represented a newly pluralistic city. His characters weren't broad symbols for what it meant to fit in; they were people challenging the idea of fitting in in the first place.

The collection's signature story, "Blight," is narrated by one of those Poles, a young man recalling the moment when his neighborhood, Pilsen, was deemed an "Official Blight Area" by the mayor. For a person with few interests beyond the White Sox and comic books, and who sees then-mayor Richard J. Daley as a distant, kingly figure, the idea of his turf having an official status—and a low-class one at that—is at once revelatory and baffling to him and his friends:

"How can a place with such good viaducts have blight, man?" Pepper asked…

"Frankly, man," Ziggy said, I always suspected it was a little fucked up around here."

"Well, that's different," Pepper said. "Then let them call it an Official Fucked-Up Neighborhood."

It's a joke, but Dybek makes it clear something serious has changed: the boys have been told they're now outsiders twice over, ethnically and civically. It's as if the maps in their textbooks have been replaced with something new, in unfamiliar shapes. They're forced to learn a new language—the story turns on multiple attempts to define "blight"—and their wisdom no longer arrives solely through an immediate social circle of family, church, school, and friends. Now, they're reckoning with being a function of the dictates of Da Mare.

The boys catch a sense of just how much they've been "placed" when they visit the tonier Oak Street Beach: after taking in "the white-sailed yachts" and "the lake-reflecting glass walls of high rises," they return home joking, "Back to blight." The term becomes at once a badge of honor and a source of resentment. The band they form starts out as the No Names but soon becomes the Blighters, because "there seemed to be some unspoken relationship between being nameless and being a loser." But the pathos of the story is the creeping knowledge that being a Blighter is being a loser, too. The choice is to embrace the term ironically or to ignore it. But agreeing with Mayor Daley's dictate is not an option.

Jeffrey Eugenides gives Dybek's vision of place and individualism a broader scale; his talent has long been to track this sense of disassociation and give it a more portentous, even epic scope. His debut novel, *The Virgin Suicides* (1993), sketched out the demises of three attractive young girls in the Detroit suburbs in lush, ironic prose; in 2011's *The Marriage Plot*, he merged semiotics and Austen to follow the paths of a woman and two suitors starting from their lives as Brown University undergrads. But his greatest achievement remains his second novel, 2002's Pulitzer-winning *Middlesex*, which is not just a rich study of gender but a sophisticated exploration of the immigrant experience in Detroit during its mid-century industrial heyday.

Cal (born Calliope), the novel's hermaphrodite narrator who is the daughter of Greek immigrants, discovers her male aspect as a teenager. Eugenides emphasizes the tension between Cal's inbetween, uncertain status and the rigidity of Cal's surroundings—Detroit's hard-line class distinctions (especially between lower-class Greeks and upscale WASPs) and the rigors of the assembly line. There's a rhetorical tension too, upending the conventions of the bildungsroman and the Homeric ode. "Sing now, O Muse, of the recessive mutation on my fifth chromosome!" Cal writes in the opening pages, as if he were writing a mock-*Odyssey*. "How it blew like a seed across the sea to America, where it drifted through our industrial rains until it fell to earth in the fertile soil of my mother's own Midwestern womb."

The point of this tension is that no identity is secure — not "Detroiter," not "manufacturing," not "boy," or "girl." Detroit is a testing ground for Cal, a place where her (and his) identity is tested, shaped, and defined. It's actually an excellent setting for having your identity called into question, Eugenides suggests. "Historical fact: people stopped being human in 1913," referring to how the assembly line mechanized workers, right down to their DNA. "The adaptation has been passed down: We've all inherited it to some degree, so that we plug right into joysticks and remotes, to repetitive motions of a hundred kinds." The mid-century Midwest can try to force you to snap into a role; *Middlesex* is a late-century reminder that not everybody fit.

A novelist who challenges the rules of the assimilation narrative doesn't always get appreciated for it, though. Consider the case of **Aleksandar Hemon**, whose biography has become a kind of Midwestern literary legend. In 1992 Hemon visited Chicago as part of a cultural exchange program with his native Bosnia, where he was a young journalist, critic, and art-scene provocateur. While in the city, he experienced a spectacular case of bad timing: war broke out in his homeland during the trip, trapping him in a large, unfamiliar place where he had few contacts and didn't know the language. The need to adjust was pressing: "Converting Chicago into a personal space became not metaphysically essential but psychiatrically urgent as well," he wrote.

From there, an oft-repeated origin story proceeds: Hemon worked odd jobs (he was perhaps the worst Greenpeace canvasser ever), he picked up the language, he assimilated, he began to write fiction about his experience, and with surprising speed he became widely acclaimed for it. In 2004 he received a "genius grant" from the MacArthur Foundation (based in Chicago, as if to prove that he and the city were meant to be). Much of his fiction echoes his experience: his first story collection, 2000's *The Question of Bruno*, and his debut novel, 2002's *Nowhere Man*, feature an alter ego, Jozef Pronek, who strains to find a place in American society.

Yet there's a disconnect between Hemon's real-life story, which in profiles and reviews typically reads as European-refugee-makes-good, and Hemon's fiction, which makes the immigrant experience a more complicated affair. In *Nowhere Man*, for instance, an ESL class chants an English lesson that's a comic indictment of American attainment: "I have never read *Moby-Dick*. I have never seen the Grand Canyon. I have never been in New York. I have never been rich." And though he often writes about the city affectionately, Chicago isn't a setting for Hemon so much as a launchpad to explore placelessness and disconnection. That mood is sometimes motivated by history, as in his 2008 novel, *The Lazarus Project*, inspired by the true story of a Jewish immigrant killed by the Chicago police, sparking a wave of xenophobia. Or it can play out as comedy, as in 2015's *The Making of Zombie Wars*, a novel that uses the undead as a metaphor for otherness. Or it plays out in heartbreak, as in "The Aquarium," an essay about the death of his infant daughter in which he fumes at faith, medicine, and family. Hemon became an American less by choice than by force, by accident, which gives his prose a seriousness and skepticism—he typically writes about America not from the perspective of constitutional idealism, but decay and threat. For his heroes, America isn't the New World but the Old World's postwar absurdity in a different costume.

In that regard, Hemon has a compatriot in the Egyptian writer **Alaa Al Aswany**, whose 2008 novel, *Chicago*, imagines the lives of a handful of Egyptian students and teachers at a Chicago medical school. Compared to their homeland, America is a place of opportunity and small but meaningful freedoms. (Including unapproved ones: one student hastens to procure a prostitute upon his arrival.) But the new arrivals haven't quite escaped the dictatorial regime in Egypt, and Al Aswany suggests that they can't resist looking through Chicago through that filter: the pocket history of Chicago that opens the novel characterizes the Great Fire of 1871 not as a cataclysm that allowed a new city to re-emerge Phoenix-like, but as a place of shantytowns filled with people laboring on behalf of the millionaires who could afford the new high rents. "The American capitalist system was able, as usual, to present a temporary solution to the crisis," he writes. That is, it rebuilt itself after the fire but failed to create a sustainable environment for those who struggle under that system.

Dinaw Mengestu is similarly attuned to the ways that global dysfunction feeds into domestic displacement. Mengestu, another MacArthur fellow, was born in Ethiopia, raised in central Illinois, and attended Georgetown University. His time in Washington, D.C. provided the setting for his first book, 2008's *The Beautiful Things That Heaven Bears*, an assimilation novel whose twist is that its young immigrant hero is navigating not one, but two, cultures, his rough-edged neighborhood of D.C. and the tonier power culture he observes working in a restaurant. Since then, his books have been largely set the Midwest, dwelling more on the countries left behind and how difficult it is to form enduring relationships amid that tension. His 2010 novel, *How to Read the Air*, focuses on Jonas, who works in a firm helping to provide asylum for refugees—a job that usually requires the spinning of lies, large and small, in order to help move people through the system. In the process, Jonas uses his father's death as a prompt to think about his own history. Mustn't he know something about the plight of Africans, even though he was raised in Peoria, Illinois? Shouldn't he have exotic tales to tell about his past, even though he's a diffident schoolteacher? In Jonas's eyes, the world demands coherent narratives, a point driven home to him at his former job helping amnesty applicants. There, he was responsible for taking their histories and "pointing out places where some stories could be expanded upon for greater narrative effect."

For Jonas, who's trying to obscure a past he doesn't know for certain and who fabricates to just keep his life in motion, a Midwestern background is a perfect cover — nobody challenges it. His ex-wife tells him, "Talk to any immigrant long enough and they'll tell you where they came from, and then once they start most of the time they won't really want to stop…. But the most anyone can get out of you is that you were born in the Midwest. Most of the time you don't even say the city. Just the Midwest, as if that means anything."

The Midwest's liminal qualities also echo personal detachment in his third novel, 2014's *All Our Names*. Set in the 1970s, the story turns on Isaac, a Ugandan war refugee who's arrived in the downstate Illinois town of Laurel, where he falls for a do-gooding caseworker, Helen. She falls for him too, but their relationship is challenged early on, thanks to the racist locals who tacitly communicate their contempt for the couple when they go on a lunch date. The locals' inability to come right out and say what they're feeling is worse than any variation of "Midwestern nice" to Helen, who thinks, "We weren't divided like the South and had nothing to do with any of the large cities in the North. We were exactly what geography had made us: middle of the road, never bitterly segregated, but with lines dividing black from white all over town." But as in Mengestu's other novels, the city provides an escape hatch, a place where the two can be coupled — not assimilated, exactly, just less scrutinized. But that's enough: indeed, Chicago is depicted as so nurturing that even the buildings are tender. The two head to the John Hancock Tower downtown and touch it in the closing pages. "I wanted to say it was softer than I expected," Helen says.

The feeling of disassociation isn't exclusive to immigrants from other countries—as race reshapes neighborhoods, stories become more complicated for people who've been settled in for generations. Black and white tensions remain pervasive, but also indirect; whites hasten to the cover of the internet to process their confusions. Which is why we now have the Great American Neighborhood Listserver Novel. *What We've Lost Is Nothing*, the 2014 debut of **Rachel Louise Snyder**, explores black and white divides in Oak Park, Illinois, a Chicago suburb that's struggled to be more integrated than the city that shadows it. (Snyder once worked as a resident manager in a program that promoted integration in apartments there.) Oak Park, a relatively tony suburb that claims Ernest Hemingway and Frank Lloyd Wright as famous residents, abuts the predominantly black Austin neighborhood of Chicago. That's the crux of the conflict: in Snyder's novel, the white Oak Parkers stand ready to accuse black Austin residents for any local crimes, even as they claim their progressive bona fides. Snyder is savvy about "I'm not racist, but…" chatter that proliferates online: "I like a diverse population as much as anyone here, but we're kidding ourselves if we don't think this was perpetrated by at least SOME west siders." Pointedly, the crime that drives the novel's plot (and the online action) occurs on Ilios Lane—Troy, a city under siege.

Snyder explores a variety of divisive forces: policing, culture, schools, and especially housing and redlining and restrictive covenants. It doesn't take much to surface the anxieties that are concealed by the white residents there. "Oak Park had caught the disease of the country at large, the post-9/11 pandemic that took over hearts, minds, logic, the reason and compassion of people who, just a day, a week, a month earlier believed themselves free of prejudice."

Taken together, these writers have unpacked, undone, and revised the traditional assimilation story. The assumption is no longer that people will find a way to get along together in a community, but carve out an individual niche. The expectation of conformity is avoided, if not actively resented. Hemon openly voices his skepticism about the American narrative—his characters' paths in Chicago are less freestyle and more tentative. Jeffrey Eugenides recognized how our very bodies can protest being slotted into expectations. Al Aswany and Dybek's heroes are immigrants or their second-generation offspring who aspire to the middle class but are made keenly aware of how circumscribed their movements are. *What We've Lost Is Nothing* reveals how blacks are exploited or neglected by white fear, either casually voiced in conversation or enacted into law.

In a 2013 interview with the *Rumpus*, Hemon questioned the big-shouldered, broad-lawned, accommodating reputation of Chicago—the idea that its size allows it to be inclusive, that its infamous grid system of streets made it easy to navigate and thereby easy to assimilate. "Chicago has very few public spaces where people are encouraged to get together," he says. "It's partly to prevent riots, and also to segregate a city with a history of racial segregation…. Sarajevo and European cities are not designed the way Chicago is, like a grid. They tend to go out of the city center concentrically."

Even so, Hemon plainly loves Chicago: His 2013 nonfiction collection, *The Book of My Lives*, includes an essay titled "Reasons Why I Do Not Wish to Leave Chicago: An Incomplete, Random List," which rhapsodizes about L stops and the color of Lake Michigan and "young Bucktown mothers carrying yoga mats on their backs like bazookas." But you never lose the feeling that Hemon's love was labored for in unconventional ways; his love is born of distaste. His love is born out of recognition of the official fucked-up neighborhoods, in spite of the system, out of recognition that the system was rigged against many people in a way that's built right into the geometry of the streets.

IS THIS HEAVEN?

For many readers, the contemporary Midwestern religious novel has a single shining exemplar: **Marilynne Robinson**. (Indeed, for many she's the shining exemplar of the American religious novel, or the American novel, period.) Robinson grew up in Idaho, the setting for her debut novel about three troubled sisters, 1980's *Housekeeping*, and when she moved to the University of Iowa to teach at its landmark Writers' Workshop, her fictional settings joined her: the three novels she's written since then, *Gilead* (2004), *Home* (2008), and *Lila* (2014), concern the lives of two aging preachers, their families, and their extended histories in the state. That a somber Calvinist who writes measured fiction and scholarly essays on religion has become one of the country's most beloved novelists seems an unlikely twenty-first century phenomenon. But as the critic Briallen Hopper suggests, Robinson has a knack for making theological-minded literary fiction palatable to wide swaths of readers, religious and not: "She evokes the hope of heaven in the everyday, and the promise of baptismal blessing in ordinary water," she writes.

Critics respond to Robinson's duality by framing her as a secular saint, an Iowa abbess delivering profundities in humble dress. In a review of *Gilead* in the *New York Times Book Review*, James Wood credited Robinson for blending religious concerns with a plainspoken diction, celebrating "the care with which Robinson can relax the style to a Midwestern colloquialism" in a moment when a storm "lifted the roof right off" a henhouse.

I'm not sold on the notion that "lifted the roof right off" qualifies as a regional colloquialism. But Wood's observation is indicative of something peculiar about the praise Robinson receives. For many critics, lauding the supposed plain-spokenness of her prose—or her religiosity—often is a way to elide her darker thematic concerns. Diane Johnson, for instance, calls out the "wonderful feel for Midwestern life" in *Lila*, a novel about "faith" and "goodness, a property Midwesterners like to think of as a regional birthright." Roxana Robinson called *Lila* a "quintessentially American story: set in the deepest Midwest, peopled by humble characters, centered on family, driven by hope."

Such assessments give short shrift to a set of novels that place the Civil Rights Movement, poverty, violence, prostitution, troubled faith, and failure at their center. Robinson herself explained that the title of *Home* wasn't meant to imply coziness or comfort: "If you say of a 45-year-old man that he has gone back home, it tends to mean that the world hasn't worked out." Indeed, very little works out for the characters in that novel: Glory, its heroine, has dead-ended in love and work, and her brother Jack, a prodigal son figure and ne'er do well who impregnated a farm girl, scandalizes the town by seeing a black woman, and seems to live to poke holes in dad's theology. Black families are unwelcome in Gilead, but Jack's father is oblivious to that fact, thinking of a church arson that ran them off as "a little nuisance fire."

As the critic Sarah Churchwell has pointed out, Robinson understands Iowa (to which *Lila* is dedicated) has long been a crucible of religious progressivism: it inspired Harriet Beecher Stowe, played a role in stoking the Civil War, and hosted stops on the Underground Railroad. That these elements are understated when Robinson's novels are discussed speaks to which elements of her novels critics choose to celebrate. Indeed, it may say something that it took more than a decade since the publication of *Home* for Hopper to point out the factual inaccuracies of the depiction of the Civil Rights Movement in *Home*, confusing the bus boycott in Montgomery, Alabama, with the police violence in Birmingham, Alabama. Robinson's main job, for many critics, is to provide a kind of secular-spiritual uplift—at the expense of the more turbulent story she delivers underneath. But they are worth visiting—or revisiting—for that.

That's a long way of saying that Robinson's novels are more irreverent about religion than they let on. But their quiet tone makes them no less a challenge to the old-school image of priests as sturdy community leaders—an image perpetuated by aw-shucks joshing on Garrison Keillor's radio show, *A Prairie Home Companion*, or the breezy crime novels of William X. Kienzle and Andrew M. Greeley featuring Catholic priests. But more heterodox writers have been around as well. Decades before Robinson wrote *Gilead*, the novelist and short story writer **J. F. Powers** pulled off a kind of variation on Robinson's strategy. Instead of foregrounding the ways the secular world beats a path to the door of well-intentioned, if somewhat distant, Protestant priests, Powers's Catholic clergymen were city slickers who approached their faith out in the world and often more alive in secular than spiritual spheres. "His priests are small people in a big world," as the critic Denis Donoghue put it.

This tension—acknowledging a vow to be a good Christian while resisting its doctrinal fetters—implies seriousness, if not sanctimony. But Powers's excellent 1962 debut novel, the National Book Award-winning *Morte d'Urban*, is largely a comic novel, and its humor is embedded in the ways its spiritual servants are as subject to office politics, flirtation, and creature comforts as the average office drone. (Indeed, the novel also qualifies as the rare entertaining novel about business and work life.) Its hero, Father Urban, is a leader among the Clementines, a fading order in the Midwest. After falling out of the monsignor's favor, Urban is banished from his comfortable perch in Chicago and reassigned to a retreat in rural Minnesota ("the latest white elephant") where his presence is barely tolerated, if not actively resented, by the locals. Upon his arrival in the fictional town of Deusterhaus, the train station agent doesn't pay what Father Urban considers the appropriate attention. But the town is disinterested in kiss-the-ring gesturing: "An old dog lying behind the counter woke up and gave him a look that said, Can't you see he's working on his report?" His religious cohort on site is only slightly less sluggish.

Father Urban eventually balances his dueling instincts to retreat and to act out, to do the church's service while enjoying the lakes and the links—the "death" of the title, as the famed Trappist monk (and Powers admirer) Thomas Merton put it, "is the death of a superficial self leading to the resurrection of a deeper, more noble, and more spiritual personality." But even so, the very concept of a religious story being told in business-story dress was inherently subversive. Better still, as Jonathan Yardley argues, its hero was a Midwestern public figure with more wit and sophistication than blunt Babbitry. Faith may be the house of freedom, but the church is a perpetual fixer-upper: the Clementines's "history revealed little to brag about—one saint (the Holy Founder) and a few bishops of missionary sees, no theologians worthy of the name, no original thinkers, not even a scientist," Powers writes. "The Clementines were unique in that they were noted for nothing at all. They were in bad shape all over the world."

Morte d'Urban bested some tough competition for the year's National Book Award, including better-known works like Vladimir Nabokov's *Pale Fire*, Katherine Anne Porter's *Ship of Fools*, and John Updike's *Pigeon Feathers*. But despite its prize-winning status, the novel was unmistakably counterprogramming against more comfortable depictions of Midwestern clergy, and for some critics in his hometown of St. Cloud, Minnesota, the irreverence pushed too far. In a 1962 letter, Powers bemoaned the unnamed *Minneapolis Tribune* critic who criticized his "humor with a capital H." "So he called it banal ... I wouldn't mention it, but people see me on the street here and look away as if I'd been taken in adultery with a chicken."

The critic, novelist, and poet **Thomas M. Disch** was similarly dissatisfied with the pieties of the Minnesotans he grew up with. His 1979 novel, *On Wings of Song*, delivers a scathing critique of religion in the form of a science-fiction novel—but not so blistering that he doesn't grasp the value of what he's railing against. Its hero, Daniel, is a teenager capable of flying under his own power by singing, like many in the book's world. But he has the misfortune of growing up in Iowa, where the practice of singing-flying is banned by hyperconservative evangelicals known as "undergoders" who consider the skill "part of Iowa's general decline." Trips to relatively more liberal Minnesota awaken him to just how crabbed and isolated his hometown is, but acting out goes poorly: a stint making surreptitious deliveries of the *Star-Tribune* gets him sent to jail. The only solution is to get out of the Midwest entirely, and eventually Daniel makes his escape to New York.

On Wings of Song isn't the first notable science-fiction novel to satirize the heartland—Robert A. Heinlein's 1951 novel, *The Puppet Masters*, is an alien-invasion yarn that exploits the region's jus' folks sensibility. (Where better for a nefarious and squishy extraterrestrial force to disguise itself as gentle and unassuming?) Thing is, Disch's interest in faith is as considered as Robinson's, and his invective against Iowa's hard-right sensibility never goes so far as to reject faith entirely. Indeed, Daniel embraces a religion of a sort, a fake-it-till-you-make-it philosophy he learned about in prison through a book titled *The Product Is God*: "If the way we become the kind of people we are is by pretending," the book says, "then the way to become good, devout, and faithful Christians (which, admit it, is a well-nigh impossible undertaking) is to *pretend* to be good, devout and faithful."

Disch was an atheist, and while his treatment of this sophistry is mostly satirical—he'd revisit the theme in his 1994 novel, *The Priest*, about a pedophile priest—the ersatz religion also helps give Daniel the wings he hopes for. (He sincerely clings to a line of Kierkegaard's, preaching the stubbornness of faith: "purity of heart is to will one thing.") Heartland Christianity wasn't the problem for Disch so much as the calcified brand of it pushed by the "undergoders." He underscored that distinction in the novel's epigraph, which acknowledged the challenge and the inspiration of religion, that true faith meant working to escape the sanctimonious forces that try to control it: *Profiscicere, anima Chrisitiana, de hoc mundo.* Go forth, Christian soul, from the world.

If *Morte d'Urban* is relatively obscure, *On Wings of Song* has positively vanished—it's currently out of print and unlikely to inspire the handsome reissues that Powers's works have enjoyed by New York Review Books. As goes those books, so goes literary fiction about religion in general: Powers's death in 1999 effectively ended sustained literary interest in the lives of Catholic priests, or even Catholicism. (One notable exception: *Vestments*, John Reimringer's well-turned 2011 novel about a fallen Twin Cities priest.) That leaves Marilynne Robinson as the standard-bearer of the religious literary novel, prompting some critics, such as Paul Elie, to wonder whether it might be revived again. For Elie, novels like *Gilead* were admirable as fiction, but not especially innovative when it came to religion: they are, he writes, "set in the past, concerned with a clergyman, presenting belief as a family matter, animated by a social crisis."

Yet around the same time Elie was tussling with this shortcoming, critics were tussling over the faith (or lack of it) of another towering Midwestern writer: **David Foster Wallace**. Wallace was a churchgoer while he was living in Bloomington, Illinois, where he taught at Illinois State University and finished his 1996 epic novel, *Infinite Jest*. But the depth of his faith was obscure; he told interviewer David Lipsky while on tour for the book that he went to dances regularly at "Some Number Baptist Church of Bloomington" where "everyone more or less wants to leave each other alone." In the years since, Wallace's faith has largely been understood as a function of his efforts to stay sober. Snooping around Wallace's home, Lipsky found a postcard on the bathroom wall of the "St. Ignatius Prayer that sounds very much like the AA prayer." Wallace's biographer, D. T. Max, wrote that "my assumption is that this practice [of churchgoing] began after he stopped drinking and smoking pot as part of getting clean and may have continued either because he felt it centered him or merely out of habit, as part of his sense of himself as a middle-class Midwesterner."

This is a touch condescending—Max assumes an urge to belong to a class, while Wallace himself said he wanted just the opposite; church was a place where he could be left alone. It's true Wallace's writing was more concerned with ethical philosophy than faith. Yet the two weren't entirely separate spheres for him, and in one remarkable work of his, this notion finds an elegant merger.

Chapter Twenty-Two of *The Pale King*, the unfinished novel Wallace left behind when he hanged himself in 2008, is a 100-page memoir by Chris Fogle, one of the IRS agents at the center of the book's plot.* It's a road-to-Damascus tale in slacker dress: the narrator recalls his bland Chicago childhood, his drug use, and his overall lassitude until the death of his father, an accountant, motivates him to begin straightening up and prepare to enter the ranks of the IRS. He is fumbling badly for a sense of self-awareness when he accidentally sits in on a tax class taught by "one of DePaul's few remaining Jesuit professors, meaning with the official black-and-white clothing ensemble and absolutely zero sense of humor or desire to be liked or 'connecting' with the students." The theme of reconciliation with the father is plain,

---

*The chapter has been published by Madras Press in a standalone edition titled *The Awakening of My Interest in Advanced Tax*. Proceeds benefit Granada House, a halfway house near Boston where Wallace spent time in 1989 when recovering from addiction.

partly because Fogle so strenuously denies his father's role in inspiring him to pursue tax accounting.

Before what he calls his "conversion," Chris's attitude toward Christianity was defiantly smug—he writes of being nineteen (his pre-"wastoid" years) and mocking a young born-again woman. But the grown-up Chris, bolstered by the IRS gospel, is willing to accommodate the girl's revelation: "It's true that her story was stupid and dishonest, but that doesn't mean the experience she had in the church that day didn't happen, or that its effects on her weren't real." (There are echoes here of Disch's pragmatic approach to faith, and of the heroine of Robinson's *Lila*, who escaped homelessness and prostitution and picks up the Good Book as much to vet the intellect of the preacher who has his eye on her as to connect with God.) Regardless, Chris's own experience is a revelation in itself: he's intellectually seduced by a professor who "had a kind of zealous integrity that manifested not as style but as the lack of it."

That professor's speech, like many sermons, is a call to find life and spirit in a world of pain and drudgery. "I wish to inform you that the accounting profession to which you aspire is, in fact, heroic…. Enduring tedium over real time in a confined space is what real courage is." As the speech grows in intensity—indeed, Wallace gives it homiletic rhythms—he intones: "Gentlemen, you are called to account." Chris walks away "in a strange kind of hyperaware daze, both disoriented and very clear." He soon joins the IRS, which he calls "entering the Service."

The Jesuit substitute is something of a comic figure, surreal in his righteousness about the bland world of accounting. His punning invocation about being called to account is evidence enough of that. But *The Pale King* as a whole is serious about the business of boredom—How do we live with it? Can we transcend it?—and Chris Fogle's story is as sincere a conversion narrative as anything in Marilynne Robinson's fiction. There is a reflex among critics to see a novel about religion in the Midwest and perceive it as a repository of homespun wisdom, gently delivered; the *Guardian* review of *Lila* promised a return to "Robinson's quiet Midwest" — a place, Robinson wanted us to know, that was filled with racially motivated church burnings, prostitution, hard labor, and other physical suffering. But writers in the center of the country have been looking for a different way of perceiving faith. In the IRS, Wallace imagines an echo of the Midwestern church of anonymity he cultivated in his own life, a place where the faithful found a community, but one where they could also be left alone.

HARD WORK AND OTHER LIES
OF THE HEARTLAND

Indoctrination into the Midwestern ideology of hard work starts early.

Growing up where I did (the industrial near-west Chicago suburbs) and when I did (the late 1970s and early 1980s) I was conditioned to think of **Laura Ingalls Wilder**'s books as tales from a distant continent, if not a different solar system: they were stories that happened far away from me, and written for girls. The girls I went to school with must have been partly charmed by *Little House on the Prairie*, the hit TV show that followed the adventures of a sweet-tempered farmgirl in rural Minnesota. But in truth those books deliver the core message of redemption by labor that's defined the Midwestern mythos for decades; it's the territory that defined the region before Midwestern cities grew in ways that complicated their borders. And it's where readers (and later viewers) retreated when those complications actively defied the definition of "Midwest" in the public imagination.

The action in the first book in the Little House series, *Little House in the Big Woods* (1932), takes place in Pepin, Wisconsin, tucked in the middle left of the state's baseball glove, on the banks of the Mississippi River. But though there's action, there's little semblance of a plot: the book is almost entirely about everyday tasks. There is no core plot to speak of, unless "survival" counts as one. There's little, too, in the way of character development. Animals are tracked and killed for meat that's smoked and stored so the family can make it through the winter. Young Laura helps with baking and churning. She and her sister help make bullets for daddy's gun. They gather sap for maple syrup. Firewood is chopped, horses are tended to, grain is harvested. Ingalls's goal is to describe the *processes* of life on the settlement, and the sole arc is the year-long changes that the climate demands of the family.

Wilder was plainly aware she was writing for children who might have limited patience for quotidian details about homesteading—the book is seasoned with vignettes about dances and Christmas presents and Pa playing his beloved fiddle, as well as the fantastic interludes that Pa delivers about his encounters with deer and bears and panthers. But Wilder never lets her readers forget that these are interstitial moments in the narrative, breaks from the hard business of survival. Pleasure is where you find it in this place, and sometimes it's found after slaughtering a pig:

> When the water was boiling they went to kill the hog. Then Laura ran and hid her head on the bed and stopped her ears with her fingers so she could not hear the hog squeal.
>
> "It doesn't hurt him, Laura," Pa said. 'We do it so quickly.' But she did not want to hear him squeal.
>
> In a minute she took one finger cautiously out of an ear, and listened. The hog had stopped squealing. After that, Butchering Time was great fun.

With the first *Little House* book appearing during the heart of the Great Depression, Wilder had hit a nerve. "Hard times whet the appetite for survival stories," the critic Judith Thurman wrote in an essay on the Little House series for the *New Yorker* that elaborates on how Wilder and her daughter, Rose Wilder Lane, used the series in part to reflect their libertarian and conservative values. (Ronald Reagan said the TV show was his favorite; Sarah Palin was reportedly a childhood fan of the books.) It may be that the hardscrabble life of the Ingalls family has done more to underscore *hard work* as the root of Midwestern life. Your work isn't just "what you do," it's part of your character. And in the *Little House in the Big Woods*, work is practically the lead character.

But as long as there have been stories about the edifying elements of hard work, there have been satires and polemics about its false promises. In Richard Wright's *Native Son* (1940), Bigger Thomas's work as a chauffeur for a wealthy white family is only a source of anxiety, leading to manslaughter, despair, and prison. In Upton Sinclair's *The Jungle* (1906), the Chicago stockyards are infested with graft, disease, and workers kept under the thumb of capitalist slave drivers, forcing decent men into criminality and decent women into prostitution. In Sinclair Lewis's novels *Babbitt* (1922) and *Main Street* (1920), the upstanding, Rotary Club Midwesterners are complacent tools who've traded their humanity for cash. In Theodore Dreiser's *An American* Tragedy (1925), ambition only leaves a girl dead. Robert Coover's debut novel, *The Origin of the Brunists* (1966) was inspired by a mine disaster in central Illinois and imagined an anticapitalist movement that centered on its survivors.

The satires and critiques of work have changed with the nature of work itself. In his 2007 novel, *And Then We Came to the End*, **Joshua Ferris** sends up the conformity of big-city white-collar labor. Set in a Chicago ad agency, the novel is narrated in a collective voice that suggests uniformly desperate feelings of entrapment. (First lines: "We were fractious and overpaid. Our mornings lacked promise.") The plot turns on a planned series of layoffs that hit the firm after the dot-com boom crumbles. As employees begin dropping one by one, those who remain turn on each other to maintain their standing. In such a dehumanizing milieu, personality begins to seep out of them almost by accident, emerging in drips of gossip. One employee is writing a novel, assumed to be a "small, angry book about work"; one dead coworker leaves another a totem pole. The office devolves into petty obsessions over things like whose chairs belong to whom.

Before writing the novel, Ferris briefly worked at the global ad firm Leo Burnett, a key player in Chicago's redefined economic landscape — if the city would no longer be the center of America's manufacturing might, it could at least help sell the things made elsewhere. But Ferris knows the shift doesn't wholly compensate for what's lost, and the evidence goes beyond the layoff wildfires rampaging through the office. Workers nervously talk about how extreme workplace violence "happened only in factories and warehouses, and then only on the South Side." A highway billboard encourages people to be on the lookout for a missing girl; she's later found strangled to death, but the ad stays up because there are no other clients. "Billboards in North Aurora were good for casino boat and cigarette ads, and the occasional AIDS awareness campaign, but little else," he writes. And the satisfaction the collective "we" receives from being in a big city in tech-savvy corporate America has eroded; "we" have it no better than anybody else in the heartland. "We thought ourselves immune from things like plant closings in Iowa and Nebraska, where remote Americans struggled against falling-in roofs and credit card debt," he writes. "We were above the fickle market forces of overproduction and mismanaged inventory. What we didn't consider was that in a downturn, *we* were the mismanaged inventory."

Lionel Shriver delivers a slightly more upbeat perspective on work — though only slightly — in her 2013 novel, *Big Brother*. Shriver, an American-born author who's spent most of her adult life in England, has often used her fiction to deliver ferocious critiques of American society, from parenting to healthcare to journalism. In *Big Brother* she takes aim at American obesity and fad diets, though she's relatively tender toward the residents of the Iowa town where the novel is set. Indeed, she's affectionate about the unassuming character of the place, and she's wide awake to the state's problems with meth, extremist politics, and undocumented workers who labor in pork-processing plants reminiscent of *The Jungle*. Early on, its narrator, Pandora, admires "the modesty of the Midwest, its secure, unpretentious self-knowledge, its useful growth of crops that people ate as opposed to the provision of elusive 'services.'" The trouble is her brother, Edison, a New York jazz pianist whose weight is pushing 400 pounds.

Motivated in part by the manual labor of Iowans she sees around her—those sandbagging in advance of floods, her furniture-making husband—she's determined to get to get task-oriented about Edison's "slow-motion suicide-by-pie." She moves with Edison into an apartment and puts him on a strict diet of protein-powder shakes, a restrictive diet that diminishes his frame, tightens their brother-sister bond, and weakens her marriage.

After dropping 225 pounds in one miraculous year, Edison is a success story … until he isn't. Writing herself into a narrative corner, Pandora eventually confesses—she made up Edison's recovery. "For my hip, downtown brother to have buried himself anonymously in the middle of the country is fanciful, especially after he'd already buried himself in himself, hiding between the perimeters of his own enormity as I have hidden between coasts." Pandora is hard-working like any Iowan, but she comes to recognize that saving Edison would not have been a useful job—just the delivery of a dubious "service" that her customer didn't want. Work is valuable, but the Midwestern myth that redemption can be achieved if we just power through it can be a damaging delusion. Sometimes our bodies simply betray us.

That said, there *is* a novel about the virtue of work that plays into the mythologies of the hardscrabble, bootstrapping Midwesterner—but even it sounds a note of caution. In his 1965 novel, *Stoner*, **John Williams** imagined a steady-footed classics scholar who, raised in a Missouri farm family, heads to college to study agriculture and instead has his head turned by literature. His life, which Williams relates with a beautiful, plainspoken placidity, is one of good, serious effort undermined — by a shrewish wife, by department chairs playing office politics, and by his own hubris as he pursues an embarrassing affair with a young scholar. Even so, Stoner is proud of what works of scholarship he's produced, and he adores his students.

Williams is careful, though, not to apply a feeling of heroism to his hero. Williams avoids any suggestion that work is redeeming or spine-straightening or any of the other clichés that attach to worthy labor. On the very first page, Williams informs us of his hero's death and notes that for his older colleagues, "his name is a reminder of the end that awaits them all, and to the younger ones it is merely a sound which evokes no sense of the past and no identity with which they can associate themselves or their careers."

So much for the redemptive power of hard work. Which is exactly the way Williams wanted it. *Stoner* is a much-loved novel now, earning a second life among readers for its durability as a wrenching tale simply told. But it was a bust upon publication, and in one of the few interviews he conducted to promote the novel's release, Williams said his goal was to write a novel that was "wholly devoid of 'symbols,' and I wanted to do so out of an odd conviction that human beings are important, not because they are 'symbols of something.'" To that end, there's a lovely passage toward the end of the novel hammering home the notion that while hard work is a good thing, it's not necessarily a noble thing:

> Deep in him, beneath his memory, was the knowledge of hardship and hunger and endurance and pain. Though he seldom thought of his early years on the Booneville farm, there was always near his consciousness the blood knowledge

of his inheritance, given him by forefathers whose lives were obscure and hard and stoical and whose common ethic was to present to an oppressive world faces that were expressionless and hard and bleak.

The word "hard" appears three times in that short passage. All romantic notions of labor are scoured clean off it. Williams's hero was a Missouri bred existentialist. You put in the hours, do your best, navigate pitfalls, but there's little chance you'll be remembered or admired for it anyway.

KEEP THE MIDWEST WEIRD

I t's not surprising that so many baseball novels have been set in the Midwest—until the major leagues began grooming players from South America, Asia, and Cuba in recent decades, the stereotypical diamond prospect was an Iowa or Great Plains farm boy. And because baseball is so closely tethered to America's idealization of itself, it makes sense that so many of those Midwestern baseball novels are quasi-religious stories, origin myths manqué. Robert Coover's 1968 novel, *The Universal Baseball Association, Inc., J. Henry Waugh, Prop.*, is a religious allegory right down to the "Yahweh" reference in the proprietor's name—Waugh is the godlike mastermind of a league entirely of his own imagination. W. P. Kinsella's *Shoeless Joe* (1982), which later inspired the cozy Kevin Costner fantasy *Field of Dreams*, was an Iowa baseball fever dream complete with a Christ-like gathering of apostles, men risen from the dead, and a host of redemption themes. A lesser-known but endearingly peculiar 1984 novel, Nancy Willard's *Things Invisible to See*, featured an Ann Arbor man pitting his earthbound baseball team against one led by Death in the battle for the survival of a woman injured by an errant ball. The novel's inhabitants are a metaphysical stew of Christian Scientists, Quakers, spiritualists, freelance angels, and black Southern folk healers. More recently, Chad Harbach's

2011 novel, *The Art of Fielding*, featured a baseball prodigy at a Wisconsin college where the holy figure, oddly enough, is Herman Melville.

The tradition of the Weird Midwest Baseball novel is just a subset of a wider tradition of offbeat Midwestern storytelling, where unsettling the linguistic landscape is welcomed and even actively encouraged. After all, the region is home to the Iowa Writers' Workshop, arguably the first of the creative writing MFA programs, which claims graduates like Stuart Dybek, Denis Johnson, and Sandra Cisneros. In literary circles, MFA programs are often criticized for producing cookie-cutter writing, but they've also provided insulating spaces for unconventional writers such as Lorrie Moore (University of Michigan), David Foster Wallace (Illinois State University), and William H. Gass (Washington University). If they are feeders for what the East Coast literary magazines will publish five years from now, they are also test labs for what they'll publish ten years from now.

It may be something about the insistence that the region is so inoffensive that prompts such fierce efforts to contradict it, to rewire its syntax. The earliest example of this counterprogramming might be Sherwood Anderson's *Winesburg, Ohio* (1919), which reveals the eerie inner lives of townspeople in a series of somber "grotesques." Anderson was inspired by Edgar Lee Masters's *Spoon River Anthology* (1915), a collection of speeches by dead townspeople who'd lived in west-central Illinois, rich in secrets and hidden frustrations. The Midwest's most provocative and enduring experimentalist, though, is arguably also the region's most famous living writer. Nobel Prize recipient **Toni Morrison**'s storytelling is rich with ghosts, coincidences, and experimental wordplay. The sensibility was there from the start: Her 1970 debut, *The Bluest Eye*, is set in Morrison's hometown of Lorain, Ohio, and follows a young black girl, Pecola, who is raised to romanticize whiteness: "God was a nice old white man, with long white hair, flowing white beard and little blue eyes that looked sad when people died and mean when they were bad," she writes, in an ironic tone that at once evokes a child's speech and biblical patter. This life under the thumb of her abusive father—who rapes and impregnates her—and her obsession with being part of a white culture that wants nothing to do with her, pushes Pecola into madness, suggested first in the crazed enjambed children's lines that head chapters ("seethecatitgoesmeowmeowcomeandplaycomeplaywithj ane") and then further in the breakdown of language that closes the novel.

Morrison's language reflects the commingling of cultures in the Midwest, the way blacks who'd moved to the region in search of a better life set old folkways against entrenched racism; in *Song of Solomon* (1977) the language is at once biblical, blunt, and magical-realist. And perhaps more than any other contemporary writer, Morrison has understood the fuzziness of the Midwest's borders, the way southern Ohio becomes more truly Southern. In her 1987 novel, *Beloved*, she describes the Ohio River valley as "territory infected by the Klan. Desperately thirsty for black blood, without which it could not live, the dragon swam the Ohio at will."

Morrison's linguistic slipperiness inspired a generation of African-American authors, but not exclusively. **Laird Hunt**, for instance, inherited Morrison's sense of blurring and experimentation in his 2003 novel, *Indiana, Indiana*, a remarkable effort to apply the Modernist Lit playbook to the heartland. Its hero, Noah, is an elderly man tormented about his decision to institutionalize his wife, Opal. The fragmented backstory is rich in half-lit imagery of arson, flames, flickering movies, and contrasts of light and dark: "In the summer, timothy, Queen Anne's lace, goldenrod, and morning glories grow up around the collapsing tractor, and one sun-glazed afternoon last August as they were walking past it, Max said, looks like you have grown yourself a burning bush." Some of the language is nakedly Faulknerian ("I will be a fisherman for Christ, then, after a few minutes, I will be a fish for Christ, then, simply, though screaming it, I will be a fish"). But it's more correct to say that the novel's inspiration is more biblical-modernist, from its references to its doomy, thundering proclamations. "Away from the junk-cluttered room on the north end of the shed on the north side of the farm in the center of the country in the center of Indiana in the heart of the country, and down a long dark hallway toward a brightly colored door." The novel evokes place less through descriptions of the flatness of the territory, but by evoking a desolation that echoes it.

Experimentation needn't always be so somber and serious, though. **Dean Bakopoulos**'s 2015 novel, *Summerlong*, is a gleefully provocative un-Marilynne Robinson romp set around Iowa's Grinnell College, where the stifling heat has made the locals boozy, stoned, promiscuous, and eager to break free of the strictures of cornfield life. ("Armistead Maupin's San Francisco teleported to the Midwest," as *Kirkus Reviews* put it.) Don, a real-estate agent, is married to Claire, a Manhattan-raised novelist blocked on her follow-up book. They have two kids and an unhappy marriage that prompts a lot of betrayals: Don falls into the arms of a student nicknamed ABC, while Claire gravitates toward Charlie, an actor and son of an esteemed professor who only barely cloaked his career-long lecherousness. The overall trajectory is toward acting out, be it via sex, drugs, or neglect of adult responsibility, and the mood is of something in the air pushing them toward it. When Charlie arrives, the Midwest is "the world of the practical, the realm of easily achieved and sensible to-do lists." But undone by lusts, Claire is desperate for release. "When Charlie arrived she could do things like pour champagne on his belly and smoke weed and watch porn and yell at him: *Eat my pussy* or *fuck me hard* or *I'm gonna suck your big cock* and she'd yell when she came because who the fuck cared. She'd be the Lindsay Lohan of Midwestern moms for one month." It's a sultry successor to John Updike's *Couples*, except this time the women are allowed to indulge their cravings, too.

But for all of Morrison's stature and the universe of weird and woolly writers in the region, the most consistently determined Midwestern experimental writer must be **William H. Gass**. Where some offbeat writers are merely serious, Gass is downright dark: "I write because I hate," he once said. "Hard." In an afterword to his 1966 debut novel, *Omensetter's Luck*, Gass is largely given to complaining about the theft of an early draft of the novel by a colleague at Purdue University, and concludes that "I may still carry his murder in my heart."

But perhaps he's just echoing the sardonic mood of the book he wrote. Set in 1890s Ohio, the novel is a fable about religious conflict and the nature of goodness. Omensetter, the laborer of the title, is on the side of the angels, but the book is all but hijacked by the narrator of the longest section, Jethro Furber, a preacher with a habit of making tourettic, blasphemous pronouncements that seem to turn the King James Bible inside out:

"God cast His shadow over him; he was divine in his darkness."

"Tell me: how did Jesus pee? Who will preach on this point? ... Did He? Oh yea, Sisters and Brothers, He did. He peed the same as you do."

"I shall pee you like rain on a window. I shall dissolve, disperse... The Lord shall bless my labor. I shall shit you like shavings."

The mid-1960s were an odd time for a novel suffused with so much faith-mocking fury—at a moment when faith in America was transforming through the Civil Rights Movement and progressive priests like Malcolm Boyd and Thomas Merton, religion had an increasing reputation as part of a progressive solution, not as the problem. Between its setting and its sensibility,

Omensetter's Luck seemed old-hat at the time. "The world with which Mr. Gass works here has long been exhausted, you would think, not only by Sinclair Lewis but by the likes of Sherwood Anderson and Edgar Lee Masters," wrote Frederic Morton in his review of *Omensetter's Luck* in the *New York Times.* "Certainly all the hip little novelists nowadays have abandoned it for the chic regions of drug addiction and alcoholic trauma, jet-set sodomy and the dropout's novel of ideas."

But what sets Furber off (and presumably Gass, too) is a kind of timeless resentment of the region's pieties. The reverend can't abide the arrival of one Brackett Omensetter, a settler with an urge toward hardworking simplicity, but he's also voicing a cri de coeur about the nature of existence itself. Gilean, Ohio, is "dead ground" for him, and a place of "mud and running ruts" from rain, and he's deeply resentful of his assignment. "The church never moved him up," he fumes. "Left him to rot in this hole in Ohio."

Gass leaves very little room for the redemptive upbeat ending. The story's good news is ironic: Furber eventually succumbs to "a kind of joint pneumonia and madness," which brings a touch of sunlight into Gilean. But there's little question who the most important and vibrant character in the novel is: Furber's section is much longer than the other two sections of the book, as if to suggest that all these dark thoughts represent the true core of life in this glum parcel of the Midwest.

And because he has a way of articulating that feeling, Gass suggests, Furber is more noble than the purportedly heroic Omensetter is. "In my books, if anybody gets to be the hero, he's got the best passages," Gass told the *Paris Review* in 1977. "Furber is what the book turned out eventually to be all about. That's not quite right. It's rhetoric the book is about ... It's more completely, more single-mindedly about rhetoric ... Omensetter is certainly not the major figure because he is basically a person without a language. He is a wall everybody bounces a ball off. Now anybody who emerges in my work with any strength at all is somebody who has a language, and that's why he's there."

Gass has had a peculiar life in letters. In his essays and nonfiction, he typically delivers crystal-clear (if still impassioned) commentaries on literary culture, language, and metaphor. But in his fiction he's been more actively freewheeling, allowing his obsessive characters free reign to fulminate. In Gass's patch of Ohio, the character with the best words, the angriest and weirdest words, is the one who gets the last word.

SOMEHOW FORM A FAMILY

The starkest, book-length portrait of the Midwestern family I know of isn't a work of reportage, sociology, or fiction. It's a coffee-table book full of creepy family photos.

The proximate subject of Michael Lesy's 1973 book, *Wisconsin Death Trip*, is the lives and deaths of residents of the small town of Black River Falls, Wisconsin, in the late 1800s. But if the book were merely an assemblage of photographs of the war dead à la Matthew Brady, or portraits of grieving widows, the book wouldn't have survived the way it has. What's memorable—and unsettling—about the book is the way its images of loss and suffering, knitted together with contemporary news reports of domestic tragedy, presented as ordinary elements of everyday life. "The pictures you are about to see are of people who were once actually alive," Lesy writes at the start of his haunting introduction, and there they are: dead infants lay in tiny coffins like parcels awaiting shipment. Wild-eyed men and women gaze into the camera as if pleading for release. Hooded women, their backs turned to the camera, suggest an eerie, morbid tale. The book is interspersed with news items about murder, suicide, fraud, arson, disease, poisonings, and other somber goings-on in the quiet territory between Milwaukee and Minneapolis. One typical snippet reads, "The 60-year-old wife of a farmer in Jackson,

Washington County, killed herself by cutting her throat with a sheep shears."

Wisconsin Death Trip is as bracing a reminder of the perils of looking at the past as "the good old days" as any book you might read. Once again, this region is not what it seems to be — or what people say it is. And its unorthodox perspective on family and community is so enduring and potent that it inspired a pair of fine novels.

Stewart O'Nan's 1999 novel, *A Prayer for the Dying*, packs the morbid themes of Lesy's book into one downhearted character, Jacob, who's saddled with the job of sheriff, undertaker, and pastor in a small Wisconsin town. A Civil War veteran, he handles the business of caring for the ill and murdered with a steely calm — O'Nan beautifully inhabits the discomfiting *normalcy* of constant physical decline that Lesy evoked in his book. But unlike Lesy, O'Nan doesn't want to put the reader at a distance from it: the book is written in the second person, putting the reader in the role of caretaker and father figure in the ironically named town of Friendship. And O'Nan is also slightly more tender-hearted: the story turns in part on his discovery that his infant daughter is one of the townspeople who have fallen ill. As he quietly saws the boards that will form his daughter's coffin, he doubts the God he's supposed to serve: "Is it true? In all this — *after* all this — will the Lord sustain us?" But what is there to do but keep sawing? "'It's not your place to ask that,' you say, and the blade neatly cleaves the cedar in two." As an illness consumes both his family and community, forcing it under quarantine, the tragic beauty of the book is in Jacob's efforts to keep things together; O'Nan recognized that what's so arresting about Lesy's book isn't the sense of things dying and falling apart, but the town's efforts to remain standing.

Where O'Nan found a dark but humane portrait of a family in Lesy's work, **Robert Goolrick** discovered something more macabre and playfully melodramatic. *Wisconsin Death Trip* didn't just inspire Goolrick—he was "set on fire" by it, he writes in the afterword of his 2009 novel, *A Reliable Wife*, which is set in the fictional Lesy County. For Goolrick, Lesy's book was a rejoinder to the received wisdom about the nature of the rural Midwest. "We had imagined the cities to be teeming with moral turpitude and industrial madness, and rural America to be sleeping in a prosperous innocence, filled with honest and industrious people," he writes. "Not so."

A Reliable Wife's early-twentieth-century gothic tale centers on Ralph, a wealthy industrialist who has had his mail-order bride, Catherine, delivered to his Wisconsin manse. Goolrick foreshadows the coming moral haziness by casting the place in fog early on: "In the sharp weather, everything blurred, the edges disappeared leaving only vague unknowable shapes, and she was afraid." Soon enough, Catherine, resentful of the isolation her new life has thrust upon her, plots an escape by taking Ralph's adopted son as a lover and slowly poisoning her benefactor. (After regular doses of arsenic, "his eyes were black as the ice on the Wisconsin River, and just as cold.") The drama of the novel is Catherine's conflict—between the affection she might have for Ralph, and the sense that she can exploit it, that she was sold a bill of goods. Even so, Goolrick delivers a happy ending, though he's challenged the definition of what a happy ending might be, suggesting that a marriage is not so much a product of love that is then intensified and pursued, but is a cohabitation tested, Job-like, in a relentlessly unforgiving landscape. In any event, it's certainly nobody's idea of a conventional rural Wisconsin marriage.

The landscape in **Angela Flournoy**'s 2015 National Book Award-nominated novel, *The Turner House*, is more contemporary, but no less forgiving—this family is unraveling, too, amid Detroit's broken economic promises. Charles "Cha-Cha" Turner, the eldest of thirteen siblings, has spent most of his life tormented by a "haint" that he's sure he glimpsed in his home as a child.

His spectral worries are echoes of the more concrete concerns that have befallen the family. The youngest of Cha-Cha's siblings, Lelah, suffers from a gambling addiction that draws her to the shiny casinos that are desperately promoted as engines of the Motor City's revival. Troy is a police officer in a city that resents the force's lengthy response times in the wake of budget cutbacks, as well as its intractable institutional racism. (Troy's father says, "the only difference between a southern cop and a northern one was that if the northern one killed you, he would try harder to make it look like an accident.") The family home is endangered, underwater thanks to predatory mortgage rules that robbed black families' homes out from under them. There's a haint in *The Turner House*, all right, but it's real-estate finance rackets, questionable civic-growth schemes, and old-fashioned racism.

Flournoy understands as well as any novelist the way the macro influences the micro—how communities shape households—and she carefully braids institutional dysfunction with the familial. So much of the promise of the Great Migration, after all, was that if a place like Detroit couldn't eradicate racism, it could at least provide institutions—factories, civic leaders—that might allow black families to thrive despite it. Once the institutions collapsed, however, so did the families. As one character points out, one factor in Detroit's downfall wasn't so much white flight, but who was left to manage in its absence. "Hundreds of thousands of black people who were never really welcome here, a lot with no access to higher education, were essentially left to run the city," Flournoy writes. "The surrounding suburbs hadn't wanted to do business with them—they essentially boycotted the newer, blacker Detroit—which would devastate any city's economy." Flournoy is asking: What will stabilize the family and the city both when those support beams get knocked down?

Jonathan Franzen would likely be pleased that somebody is still posing the question. He is at once the best-known literary novelist of Midwestern family life, and its best-known wringer-of-hands about the purpose of such novels in the first place. In his 1996 essay in *Harper's*, "Perchance to Dream" (edited and bluntly retitled "Why Bother?" when republished in his 2002 book, *How to Be Alone*), he recalled his dilemma of wanting to write serious social novels with a regional flavor at a time when he felt mass consumerism was actively making the social novel and regionalism obsolete. "The world of the present is a world in which the rich lateral dramas of local manners have been replaced by a single vertical drama, the drama of regional specificity succumbing to a commercial generality," he wrote. "To ignore it is to court nostalgia. To engage with it, however, is to risk writing fiction that makes the same point over and over: technological consumerism is an infernal machine, technological consumerism is an infernal machine."

In light of that frustration, Franzen's challenge since he wrote those words has been to highlight that point about the infernal machine while trying to avoid being a lecturing scold about it—to mold his chosen theme into inviting novels about families and relationships. The book that helped Franzen break through his malaise, the one he produced after the appearance of "Perchance to Dream," was 2001's *The Corrections*, a stellar representation of the "tragic realism" that finally allows him to come to terms with the novel in an age of diminishing returns. The travails of the Lambert family in suburban St. Louis (pointedly renamed St. Jude) catalogues the cheap and handy ways we struggle to self-medicate our contemporary despair—drugs, sex, work, money. All of which are undone by our growing awareness of mortality, here represented by the decline of the Lambert patriarch, Alfred, from Parkinson's disease.

The Corrections is a big-picture, the-way-we-live-in-America-now novel, but it's also indelibly a work of regional fiction: the Midwest is essential to Franzen as a repository for the straightforward sensibilities that the Lambert children rebel against. For Arthur's wife, Enid, struggling to keep the family together, the Midwest represents "the only true patriotism and the only viable spirituality." But son Gary pushes back against precisely those restrictions: "What Gary hated most about the Midwest was how unpampered and unprivileged he felt in it." That attitude curdles into contempt: he "wished that all further migration to the coasts could be banned and all Midwesterners encouraged to revert to eating pasty foods and wearing dowdy clothes and playing board games, in order that a strategic national reserve of cluelessness might be maintained, a wilderness of taste." Gary is punished for his contempt, as Alfred's decline magnetizes the family.

The Corrections is a defense of "Midwestern values," but what Franzen admires about the Midwest isn't some kind of inherent homespun virtue—the extended Lamberts expose that as a lie. But what Franzen punishes Gary for is an inflexibility that's even worse than the Midwestern cliché of conformity. If you can't respond humanely to the cultural shifts around you, to the plain fact of your father's dying, you've misinterpreted the values of the place where you were raised.

Which is to say that Franzen is a believer in the Midwest, even while he's a skeptic about it.

Dialectical pondering doesn't set many hearts on fire, and his foursquare, hang-on-let's-think-about-this-for-a-minute demeanor hasn't done him many favors. His handwringing over Oprah's inclusion of *The Corrections* in her book club (retracted when the author seemed insufficiently grateful for the privilege), the lecturing tone of 2010's *Freedom*, and his complaints about online culture have made him a punching bag for many critics, particularly of the hot-take and Twitter variety. But Franzen's ambition and vision of the Midwestern novel has had an influence. That's clearest, I think, in the work of Wisconsin-born novelist

Patrick Somerville. His debut novel, 2009's *The Cradle*, involved a Midwest-wide hunt for a Civil War-era baby pram and turned into a broader novel about fatherhood; its peculiar charm was Somerville's suggestion that hustling across the landscape looking for a symbol of family can somehow produce one.

His superb 2012 novel, *This Bright River*, develops those themes into a wilder, more multivalent concoction, focused on a pair of prodigal children, Ben and Lauren, who've returned to their childhood home of St. Helens, Wisconsin. Ben is a former white-collar criminal and Lauren's medical career has hit the skids. In his lassitude, Ben is tasked by his father to spread his uncle's ashes in the Bright River, which runs by a family cabin upstate. But Somerville pushes against the easy redemption-narrative convention such a plotline suggests. The bad guy, Lauren's ex, is bad in part because of his obvious, easy contempt for the Midwest. ("Her backwater hillbilly town ... These people. Midwesterners. Good God. They may as well blow it all up, you think.") But the theme of *This Bright River* is that embracing domesticity isn't so much about embracing the values of a particular place, but being able to claim a space that is big enough for two people to redefine their own values for themselves. As it happens, a small town in the middle of Wisconsin is capable of providing exactly that.

CHILDHOOD'S END

The bildungsroman changes shape depending on where you go. On the East Coast, our young hero is typically a Gatsbyesque, I'll-take-Manhattan type, regardless of whether the hero's goal is wealth, love, or literary acclaim. On the West Coast, her goals are either the glamour of celebrity (if you're in southern California) or spiritual balance (if you're anywhere else hugging the Pacific). Such ambitions aren't radically different for the Midwesterner—after all, every person craves some mixture of attention, identity, and security while growing up. But the contemporary Midwestern bildungsroman is less individualized, less about the force of the hero's personality than the forces of place acting on them. Much like the outsiders discussed in the first chapter, these young men and women aren't out to stake a claim for anything; they're striving to find a place amid the systems trying to stake a claim on them.

William McPherson's debut novel, 1984's *Testing the Current*, is a canny and beautifully written exploration of this dynamic. Its hero is Tommy MacAllister, a pre-tween boy who lives a privileged life as the son of a Michigan industrialist just before World War II. It's an interesting time for him: he's at the midpoint between innocent enjoyment of the luxury he was born into and awareness of its consequences, and he's consistently pulled in two directions about it. Should he take a closer look at his surroundings, perhaps with the telescope he received for his birthday? Or is he better off looking inward, as his mom's gift of a kaleidoscope suggests?

Out, he decides, and what he sees is largely troubling: his mother's adultery; the chaos at his father's plant, which catches fire; a relative with a heroin habit and a double mastectomy; and, in the novel's climactic party scene, a realization of how much his extended family and friends are consumed by backbiting and racist jibes. What at first seemed like the outside world is in fact a crabbed and blinkered subclass. Tommy comes to realize that the ugliness he witnesses isn't an outlier in an otherwise sensible Midwestern existence—it's the structure he's been born into, and one he's obliged to stay with until he's old enough to make an escape. (Which he does in the novel's 1987 sequel, *To the Sargasso Sea*.) *Testing the Current* is critical of the industrial complex and aware of adultery and drug abuse in ways that would have been unspeakable in the 1930s. And McPherson is attuned to the eagerness of people at the time—especially those with appearances to keep up—to paper over their difficulties. When Tommy receives an African mask as a gift from his mother's boyfriend, he's eager to show it to his morphine addict pal, the one person he can trust to take the long view. "Take some advice from old Maxine," she tells him. "Wear it."

In **Celeste Ng**'s 2014 debut novel, *Everything I Never Told You*, stereotypes are the complicating force: set in 1970s Ohio, the book spotlights the homophobia, sexism, and racism of its time and place. James, a scholar of Chinese descent, has married Marilyn, a white Southerner. They're raising two teenagers, Lydia and Nath, in Middlewood, a college town of 3,000 residents that's largely defined by its blandness: "Driving an hour gets you only to Toledo, where a Saturday night out means the roller rink or the bowling alley or the drive-in, where even Middlewood Lake, at the center of town, is really just a glorified pond." But all is not as bland as it seems: the plot turns on that glorified pond, where Lydia is found drowned.

A place like Middlewood, Ng suggests, hastens to pass judgment on difference—life in central Ohio for James's family is effectively a parade of microaggressions before they had a name. Lydia's death, for instance, prompts a headline in the local paper titled, "Children of Mixed Backgrounds Often Struggle to Find Their Place," a news story plainly written before it was reported. James is mourning his daughter, of course, but he's also mourning the loss of what he imagined this new Midwestern frontier would be. (His academic specialty is cowboys in popular culture.) A coworker "had asked him the difference between a spring roll and an egg roll.... Only when he reached home and saw Lydia did the bitter smog dissipate. For her, he thought, everything would be different. She would have the friends to say, Don't be an idiot, Stan, how the hell would she know?" But Middlewood, it turns out, is no place to learn that lesson—Lydia is gone, and Nath is getting out entirely and going to Harvard.

For Teddy, the young hero of **Ward Just**'s 2004 novel, *An Unfinished Season*, growing up doesn't mean getting out, but it does mean growing wise to the ways Chicago functions in terms of money and class: "how the weather worked, how the rain was made, and how the rain was paid for," as Just writes. The son of a wealthy print-factory owner living in a tony suburb north of Chicago, Teddy knows his place. But he's determined to discover other places and better understand Chicago's other strata: he attends the University of Chicago in defiance of his father, who disdains the place as "the hotbed of American socialism." He explores jazz clubs in neighborhoods his cohort fear to tread. Most meaningfully, he takes a job at a newspaper, where his reporting on crime and race grates against his fellow bluebloods. But his editors, knowing his background, don't want him in their tribe either. "You better go back to Lake Forest, or wherever you come from," a city editor tells him. "Help that daddy of yours break the union."

An Unfinished Season is a well-turned coming-of-age story—Teddy, the narrator, is modeled on Just, who grew up in Winnetka and began his career as a journalist. But it's especially keen at showing the fluidity of status in Chicago, the way fortunes rise and fall thanks to shifts in politics, race relations, and the media's fits of pique. Teddy is no different: he's framed not as a striver but an unstable element, a boy with no real world to occupy. Journalism is a window into the worlds he might inhabit, but it will always be a foggy one: "I discovered soon enough that you necessarily observed from the outside and the glass was opaque."

For Marcus Messner, the hero of **Philip Roth**'s 2008 novel, *Indignation*, coming of age in the Midwest during the same era is a more visceral experience—it's not just that he's managing a tangle of anxieties about religion, morals, sex, and masculinity, it's that all those things accrue physical damage and a body count. Messner is a Jewish New Jersey native who grew up under the overly watchful eye of his father, a kosher butcher. His urge to break free from that East Coast oppression—helicopter parenting with a hatchet—prompts him, in 1951, to transfer from a local college to a conservative Christian school, Winesburg College, in northern Ohio, "eighteen miles from Lake Erie and five hundred miles from our back door's double lock."

Marcus, it turns out, has only traded one mode of repression for another—the Ohio community has its own restrictions. But the community also has its own ways of pushing back against them. Marcus protests Winesburg's demands that he attend chapel, and discovers sex with a suicidal girl whose goyishness is an additional source of angst: his mother "knew very well that by his living in the heart of the American Midwest in the middle of the twentieth century, her son was more than likely going to seek out the company of girls born into the predominant, ubiquitous, all but official American faith." So beginneth the guilt trip, though this time the wild subversive comedy of *Portnoy's Complaint* is replaced with something more piercing and dour. We know early on that Marcus has died in the Korean War, and that he wants to "reconstruct the mores that reigned over that campus and to recapitulate the troubled efforts to elude those mores." That Roth delivered this book more than a half-century after the events it chronicles implies that coming to terms with those mores remains unfinished business. The hard-line Protestants in Ohio can be just as pervasive as the "undergoders" in Thomas M. Disch's Iowa.

The anxiety of youth isn't just a theme in the works of graphic novelist **Chris Ware**—it's the necessary fuel for his narratives, and, on the evidence of his prolific output, a bottomless resource. Ware, a Chicagoan, launched his career in the early 1990s with a series of self-published comics that were as notable for their tactile features as their stories—his books came in odd publication sizes, with panels that ranged from full-color broadsheet explosions to ones that took the phrase "thumbnail sketch" literally. There's a childlike play to the format of Ware's work—his 2012 book *Building Stories* comes in a board-game-sized box, with inserts that resemble children's books. Read the actual stories, though, and such playfulness often seems like a deliberate counterweight to the gloom and despair Ware conjures.

Consider Ware's 2000 masterpiece, *Jimmy Corrigan: the Smartest Kid on Earth*, which runs on two narrative tracks. In the present day, Jimmy is a painfully insecure, loveless man who heads from Chicago for the first time to meet his father in rural Wisconsin. A parallel story follows Jimmy's grandfather, who was abused by his father. Ironies abound, from the title on down. If Jimmy is indeed the smartest kid on earth, he's had few opportunities to cultivate his intelligence. He works in a bland cubicle with blowsy coworkers; early on, he spots a man on top of a building in a superhero suit and waves cheerfully, feeling a touch of magic amid his office-drone existence. Then the man leaps to his death, revealing himself as either deluded or suicidal.

The visit with dad is awful: Jimmy's father rains down insults and abuse that forces him backward into memories of past cruelties, and Ware echoes the sentiment when the story shifts to 1898. Ware is a masterful draftsman of the style of the time; the book is lush with the calligraphic flourishes of sheet music and poster art. And his portraiture of the Columbian Exposition is exquisite, all grand, wide-panel images enlivened by architecturally precise curves and pillars and handsome statuary. But the dialogue the young boy hears is nothing but coarse — "get *up* you goddamn little son of a bitch" and "you worthless bastard," he's told, or, spotting a group of South Side blacks, "we give them their freedom and look at how they waste it." A cousin who at first seems kind heaves the same abuse on him amid the glory of the White City buildings. Ware suggests that underneath every elegant surface is a more quotidian, sadder story. Survival and glimmers of hope in the story come on the back of getting beyond family — through the deaths of the fathers. Toward the end we see images of a grand train station being demolished with a wrecking ball, a building obscured by snow. Having slayed the father, the boy is finally ready to grow up.

It's worth noting that despite this grim milieu, Ware had a happy childhood. In an interview with the *Paris Review*, Ware described his dark childhood stories as a kind of proxy for his adult disappointments. "I was trying to find a way back into making art that didn't make me want to kill myself," he says. "I felt very embarrassed and self-doubting about wanting to draw pictures that re-created the warmth of my childhood and memories of my grandparents and mom, and the usual heart-stompings and relationship disappointments that one's early twenties bring left me feeling doubly whiney and vulnerable. I found that the only thing that would fill what felt like a physical hole in my chest was writing or drawing about the pain and aloneness of life as I'd experienced it, no matter how cringeworthy." Decades prior, the St. Paul cartoonist Charles Schulz got laughs in his strip "Peanuts" by thrusting adult problems onto his pre-tween characters. Ware uses the same strategy with his youngsters—he's just chasing a different emotional effect.

BAD PLACES

Jane Smiley's three-decade-long career as a novelist often appears to be a sustained effort to demythologize the Midwest—especially Iowa, which for her is a place full of death, loss, financial ruin, affairs, and retrograde politics as much as hardworking farm families. Ironically, that demythologizing is built on mythic, millennia-old tropes; few working novelists are such intensive scholars of narrative history (her 2005 book, *Thirteen Ways of Looking at the Novel*, is a hefty but accessible study of the form), and her books are often remarkable reworkings of classic themes both in setting and structure. Her debut novel, *Barn Blind* (1980), tracks a woman with an Icarus-like obsession with horse training. Her 2000 novel, *Horse Heaven*, is a racetrack novel informed by themes in Buddhist and Christian philosophy. Her breakthrough novel, 1991's *A Thousand Acres*, transports *King Lear* to an Iowa farm, while its follow-up, 1995's *Moo*, is a French farce via a Midwestern college town. In her three-volume *Last Hundred Years* trilogy—*Some Luck* (2014), *Early Warning* (2015), and *Golden Age* (2015)—she made an epic out of Iowa, the hub of a century's worth of family drama. Regardless of the theme she chooses to work with, her assertion is consistent: big stuff happens here.

Bad stuff, too, but much as with Marilynne Robinson, critics often turn a blind eye to that. *A Thousand Acres* won the

Pulitzer and National Book Critics Circle prizes for fiction, thanks no doubt to Smiley's sharpness as an observer and the audacity of her Shakespeare-in-the-cornfields conceit. But reviewers seemed determined to frame it as dealing in homespun folk, defined by modesty and a healthy fear of the engines of wealth that function much more unselfconsciously at opposite ends of Interstate 80. Reviewing the book for the *New York Times*, Ron Carlson noted how the surrounding characters played the role of a Greek chorus, and that moreover, "there is something fundamentally Midwestern about a chorus, about all that caution." Well, sure, except Greek choruses tend to show up for tragedies and crises, which are abundant in *A Thousand Acres*—blindings, death, affairs, battling siblings, and more.

In the *Last Hundred Years*, the crises expand into a trilogy about the consequences of bad political decisions, echoed by the questionable domestic decisions its characters make. One of those consequences is climate change, which is why Iowa is an interesting setting—when the damage starts getting done (and Smiley figures it begins in earnest around 2016), we'll feel it in the cornfields, in drought-starved crops. "The soil was so dry that it had lifted off in waves," she writes. "And the Monsanto reps were nowhere to be seen, had nothing to suggest.... Record droughts in France, tornadoes in Ontario, the collapse of the oil business in North Dakota, locusts in Minneapolis paving the airport runways so that planes were grounded."

Smiley foreshadows this catastrophe in the opening pages of the first book, which reads like an unassuming sketch of Iowa farm life in the winter 1920. There's a slight breeze in the afternoon, and a farmer, Walter Langdon, notices that the snow has lasted longer than it did last year. He soon spies an owl flying by with a rabbit in its talons, seemingly presaging some kind of feral act of violence in the heartland down the line. But Smiley's opening is a feat of indirection whose purpose isn't obvious until ten imaginary decades and about 1,300 real pages later, in the closing scenes of the third book, *Golden Age*. The foreshadowing wasn't the poor abducted critter. The foreshadowing was the weather report.

Gillian Flynn's plot twists arrive a little more speedily, of course: her most famous novel is *Gone Girl* (2012), whose tale of a woman scheming to escape her failing marriage was raw meat for feminist interpretations. But a central theme in that book and its two predecessors — *Sharp Objects* (2006) and *Dark Places* (2009) — is that there's a secretly menacing quality to the Midwest that often goes unspoken. Indeed, the common thread in Flynn's work is how she exploits the flyover-country assumptions people bring to the Midwest, and her most clever twist is that the place that you — the person who picked up *Gone Girl* in an airport Hudson News — are flying over is not just more dangerous, but more complicated than you've been led to think.

In *Dark Places*, for instance, Flynn delivers a pitch-perfect satire of a quickie true-crime book about an alleged Satanic ritual killing on a Kansas farm: "Kinnakee, Kansas, in the heart of America, is a quiet farming community where folks know each other, go to church with each other, grow old alongside each other.... This is a story [about how Satanism spreads everywhere,] even the coziest, seemingly safest places." But Flynn's real-deal Kansas isn't a place that had a peculiar spasm of violence à la *In Cold Blood*. It's bad news through and through — poverty, alcoholism, busted farms. The region not only has a dark underbelly, Flynn observes, it's not especially attractive on the outside either. A scene of local billboards weave sanctimony with sex and gore: "a fetus curled up like a kitten (Abortion Stops a Beating Heart); a living room turned red from the glare of ambulance lights (Take Care Crime-Scene Cleanup Specialists); a remarkably plain woman giving fuck-me eyes to passing motorists (Hot Jimmy's Gentlemen's Club)."

Though her first novel, *Sharp Objects*, was published in 2006, all of Flynn's fiction feels Great Recessive — her Midwest is one where decades of postwar promises have gone unfulfilled. Camille, the heroine of *Sharp Objects*, is a Chicago journalist covering a pair of gruesome child murders in her hometown of Wind Gap, a village in the Missouri bootheel whose 2,000 residents are split between "old money and trash." Her editor back in Chicago keeps referring to the town as Southern, but she knows it's not that simple. "Missouri, always a conflicted place, was trying to shed its Southern roots, reinvent itself as a proper nonslave state, and the embarrassing Irish were swept out with other undesirables." That done, though, it failed to evolve from, say, 1975: "On Main Street you will find a beauty parlor and a hardware store, a five-and-dime called Five-and-Dime, and a library twelve shelves deep. You'll find a clothing store called Candy's Casuals, in which you may buy jumpers, turtlenecks, and sweaters that have ducks and schoolhouses on them."

That line would read as East Coast condescension if Flynn weren't deliberately engineering a kind of Midwestern stasis— quiet, unsuspecting, not entirely true—that provides cover for the murders, at least until a horrified Camille cracks the story open in the final chapters. Such grimness may have been on the mind of the commenter who once wrote on Flynn's Facebook page: "Can't wait to read her next book, 'Gritty People' (shortened from the original title 'Everyone in the Midwest is a Gritty Psychopath and General Bad Person')." And in the case of "Amazing Amy," *Gone Girl's* antihero, that sociopathy develops layers. In the diary she uses to frame her husband, Amy constructs isn't-this-place-boring entries about the Midwest. But once her scheme is revealed, her tone is infuriated: "The Midwest is full of these types of people: the nice-enoughs. Nice enough but with a soul made of plastic—easy to mold, easy to wipe down. The [neighbor's] entire music collection is formed from Pottery Barn compilations. Her bookshelves are stocked with coffee-table crap: *The Irish in America. Mizzou Football: A History in Pictures. We Remember*

9/11. *Something Dumb With Kittens.*" A quiet farming community where folks know each other isn't being honest, Flynn knows. But neither is *Something Dumb With Kittens.* Her own situation belies the conformity she laments.

"I'm very stubborn about the Midwest," Flynn told the *Chicago Tribune* in 2012. "To me it's great, underexploited literary terrain that's fun to roam around in. It has a strangely exotic feel to it because it's so underwritten and underused in literature." Flynn takes what's been overwritten and overused about the Midwest—the homeliness, the coziness, the politeness—and repurposes it, using the old clichés to tell a new story.

The stories of **Patrick Michael Finn** are shorter and blunter—his characters often seem ready for a bar fight—but are no less concerned with long-term damage to fading industrial towns. His two books—the 2008 novella, *A Martyr for Suzy Kosasovich,* and a 2011 collection, *From the Darkness Right Under Our Feet*—are set in 1970s and 1980s Joliet, Illinois, and capture a child's or adolescent's perspective of an industrial city that's on the verge of collapse. *Suzy Kosasovich* is a Hieronymous Bosch-like vision of a drunken teenage bacchanal that satirizes the sanctimony of the Catholic Polish neighborhood in which the titular girl lives ("she had the terrifying urge to spit all over Jesus' feet, just to make everyone hate her even more"). *Darkness* expands that imagery to a series of hard-luck types: strippers, bouncers, foster kids, and factory workers. Many stories are told from the perspective of young boys recognizing their strength for the first time: in the title story, for instance, a boy finds a creepy way to convince his abusive parents that he's not crying wolf when he says he's spotted rats in the house.

The bleakness of Finn's stories is woven through with an admirably clear-eyed sense of place, as if the troubles everyone suffers from steams up from the streets in summer. In "Smokestack Polka," he describes a wedding polka band that captures a whole region in a song: "No matter where the Jugoslavs played it, Kenosha, Oshkosh, Calumet City, Gary, or Hammond, it would always be about them, about *us*; our identical brick houses topped with green shingles; our uncles and fathers who worked in the yards, power plants, refineries, and who drank in the taverns; our grandparents who were buried in the Protection of Our Savior's Five Wounds Cemetery; our mothers who made sure we got religion, even if they didn't buy any of it themselves." In "For the Sake of His Sorrowful Passion," the imagery is cruder but memorable: "every ass in the city of Chicago takes shits that flow on down here to old Joliet."

Finn's collection arrived during a brief moment in the late aughts where two-fisted, masculine fiction was enjoying a brief revival in books like Donald Ray Pollock's *Knockemstiff*, Wells Tower's *Everything Ravaged, Everything Burned*, Philipp Meyer's *American Rust*, and Alan Heathcock's *Volt*. But the appeal of fiction for Finn isn't so much violence itself as the way it can provide a counterweight to the Midwestern script, the heterodox attitude it can express toward institutions like the neighborhood church. A key early influence, he told me, was Stuart Dybek's story "The Palatski Man." "It starts on Palm Sunday, and the kids are getting fresh palms from church and telling stories about how these are what they use to whip Jesus with," Finn says. "Which wasn't true, but I was like, 'Yeah, man. That's *exactly* what we would talk about.' All the iconography of torture that surrounds everybody in Catholicism, and that becomes part of your play."

Joliet hasn't yet generated a broad shelf of hard-luck fiction. But Detroit has acquired enough in recent years to satisfy the fictional needs of any down-at-the-heels industrial burg. The story of the collapse and strained semi-revival of the Motor City (and Flint, and other diminished Rust Belt cities) has become *the* national story about the Midwest—it's the one story the country wants to tell itself about its decline and/or rebirth when it considers flyover country.* So nearly two decades after *Middlesex*—and nearly five after Joyce Carol Oates's *them* (1970)—Detroit novels are again about what's happening now. In *You Don't Have to Live Like This* (2015), Benjamin Markovitz imagines a community where white do-gooder arrivistes in a Detroit neighborhood collide with skeptical and entrenched blacks. In *Scrapper* (2015), Matt Bell follows a scrap-metal reseller working his trade in the city's abandoned buildings.** In *The Turner House* (2015), Angela Flournoy explores the long reach of the city's declining home values on one family, and the flimsiness of economic recovery schemes that introduce as many problems at they purport to solve.

The novelist and short story writer **Bonnie Jo Campbell** was a few years ahead of the trend. Her 2009 story collection, *American Salvage*, emerged from its initial publication by tiny Wayne State University Press in Detroit to become a National Book Award and National Book Critics Circle finalist. From the first page, it's not hard to see what the critics were responding to—Campbell's blunt style, combined with the book's rural Michigan settings, suggested an inheritor of Ernest Hemingway's Nick Adams stories. But Campbell was writing from a perspective of collapse, not hale masculinity. In "The Trespasser," a family visits its rural Michigan cottage to discover the place has been wrecked by meth addicts: "A faint ammonia smell lingers, and the kitchen garbage can is full of empty Sudafed packages and the coffee filters and crumpled tinfoil." We're the stand-ins for the shocked family, confused at how such a nice place could have come to this.

---

*A pair of exceptions that use Detroit's past to explore the present: Bridgett M. Davis's 2014 novel, *Into the Go-Slow*, which is set in 1980s Detroit and tracks the beginnings of the city's collapse, is a well-made portrait of the black community there at its vibrant peak, and David Means's 2016 novel, *Hystopia,* a speculative fiction about America circa 1970, as riots consume Detroit along with much of Michigan during the Vietnam War.

**Discussing *Scrapper* at a 2016 panel at the University of Arizona, Bell observed that the novel was typically described as "realistic" or "contemporary" when he gave readings in Detroit, while on the East Coast it was called "dystopian."

Campbell's stories operate as both reportage and intimate human portraiture. An old place is sinking away, for reasons her readers might comprehend but that her characters don't always, and people have to struggle to adjust for it—or turn criminal to survive it. Campbell describes the rural Michigan settings like Kalamazoo as places that are being subsumed back into the earth: "More than half of the buildings were gone now, and there were twenty or so concrete block foundations being reclaimed by the earth out there." Schemes for retraining and revitalization are mocked as absurd—the bulk of the characters have jobs that defined a prior generation, such as machinery repairmen and janitors and salvage-yard operators. An old foundry can't become a new one: "they dissembled and dissected the equipment with torches and sold it as scrap iron in a world unprepared to reshape those materials into advanced medical machinery."

"I was writing about a recession in Michigan that maybe started ten years before it started everywhere else," Campbell told *TriQuarterly* in 2012. "Or maybe it started forty years ago, in 1970 when the auto plants started closing. Generally, fiction writers tend to be writing about material that's somewhere in the past, and it takes a long time for us to digest things. In any case, my work about what has been happening in Michigan for a while suddenly seemed relevant to what was going on everywhere. Unfortunately it seems my state isn't going to be leading the pack out of the recession."

Philipp Meyer's *American Rust* (2009) takes the message of decline to Pennsylvania's Monongahela Valley in the present day—and unlike many of his Rust Belt contemporaries, he isn't shy about reviving the kind of social commentary that marked Upton Sinclair and John Steinbeck's work. Two young men, a bad-news high-school football star and an Ivy hopeful, see their ambitions switched when one of them kills a local drifter. Amid that plot are portraits of gritty life among prisoners, trainyard workers, cops, bartenders, and doublewide denizens. The message: lacking substantial economic engines and social supports in their absence, people turn tribal. That's as true here as it is in Finn and Campbell's work, as well as in Smiley, Flournoy and Flynn — each understands the kind of ferality that bad economic times unleash in their characters, the way people become recklessly independent when institutions of work, church, and marriage collapse. Meyer is distinctive because he's more overt about it, occasionally clearing way in the narrative for declamatory statements about What the Hell Happened:

"You should have been here for the seventies, Bud. The department was buying new cruisers with Corvette engines maybe every three years. And then came the eighties, and then it wasn't just that we lost all those jobs, it was that people didn't have anything to be good at anymore." He shrugged. "There's only so good you can be about pushing a mop or emptying a bedpan. We're trending backwards as a nation, probably for the first time in history, and it's not the kids with the green hair and the bones through their noses. Personally I don't care for it, but those things are inevitable. The real problem is the average citizen does not have a job he can be good at. You lose that, you lose the country."

And the best available opportunity in the present is taking apart the past:

Poe's last big chance, strike three is what it was, dismantling work, taking apart mills and old factories, they had taken down steel mills all over the country, locally and nationally.... The work was all in the Midwest now, taking down the auto plants in Michigan and Indiana. And one day even that work would end, and there would be no record, nothing left standing, to show that anything had ever been built in America. It was going to cause big problems, he didn't know how but he felt it.

The poignancy of that passage is the sense that even-worse news is about to arrive on the heels of all that bad news—the way you see a funnel cloud you know will turn into the tornado that's going to touch down any minute now. For Jane Smiley, the trouble on the horizon is climate change, and its capacity to turn society barren and violent. In Patrick Michael Finn's Joliet, it is a diminishing faith that corrodes families and sanctions abuse and crime. In so many fictional visions of Detroit, it's a parade of "comeback" schemes that are either cynically exploitative or short-lived. And in Meyer's Rust Belt, it's a creeping feeling that the last available resource is the places that made the place live for a while, now sold for scrap. A place that's best left to memory.

THE GREAT
AMERICAN/MIDWESTERN NOVEL

The Great American Novel isn't what it used to be. When the novelist John William De Forest coined the term in 1868, the idea of a cohesive American narrative in the wake of the Civil War had obvious appeal, and through the first half of the twentieth century, there was enough jingoism and economic expansion to support the notion that the country was entitled to one. Today we recognize that America is so unsummarizable and fractured that naming a GAN is folly: such a book never existed in the first place and the critical and cultural landscape has become so atomized that nobody would ever agree on what it was anyway. *Moby-Dick*? Sweeping for sure, with plenty of adventure and much to say about obsession and hubris, but also forbidding to a casual reader. (And shouldn't an all-encompassing novel encompass many readers?) *The Adventures of Huckleberry Finn*? Mark Twain invented a folksy, ironic, distinctively American writing style, and Huck is perhaps its fullest flower, but any serious consideration of the book for GAN status crashes on the baffling plot mechanics in its final third, as it devolves into a confused farce that's arguably perpetuates the racism it comments on. Pick your novel — *Uncle Tom's Cabin* (De Forest's choice), *The Adventures of Augie March*, *Beloved*, *Gilead* — and counterarguments abound.

I come not to defend the Great American Novel, only to pay tribute to the fact that Leon Forrest also tried to write one.

And not just a Great American Novel—a great Chicago novel, a great Great Migration novel, a great coming of age novel, a spiritual novel, an experimental novel, a music novel, a comic novel, and much more besides. He tried at a time when others had all but given up, and when he himself had been all but abandoned by the literary establishment. Forrest's heaving 1992 novel, *Divine Days*, has its flaws. But it's unquestionably unfortunate that it never had a chance to become a part of the great American conversation—a predicament that's all the worse now that the novel is out of print.

A glance at the physical book will immediately explain the problem. At 1,144 pages, it is a daunting undertaking for even a determined reader; its paperback version was published by W. W. Norton, and its bulk echoes that of the publisher's famous, culture-hoovering academic anthologies. *Divine Days*'s size inevitably compromised the novel's fortunes in the marketplace: though Forrest, a Chicagoan, had published three other novels with Random House, edited and championed by Toni Morrison, *Divine Days* was published in hardcover by a small hometown publisher, Another Chicago Press, in a small run in July of 1992. That Christmas, an electrical fire in the publisher's Oak Park home destroyed many of the copies; shortly after, the press's distributor went bankrupt. In May 1993, the Chicago club the Green Mill hosted a daylong, Bloomsday-style reading from the novel to keep attention on it, culminating in a rave review by Stanley Crouch in the *New York Times Book Review,* calling it an "adventurous masterwork" and "boldly musical." In the *New Republic*, Sven Birkerts called it "a tour de force carnival of tongues." Henry Louis Gates, Jr. called it "the *War and Peace* of the African-American novel."

GAN, here we come. But though Gates's statement captures the heft and power of *Divine Days*, his praise misses the point on two fronts. First, the *War and Peace* reference implies a kind of plotiness and geographical breadth that Forrest eschewed. His story mainly centers on a pocket of Chicago's South Side, particularly the bar run by an aunt of the book's hero, Joubert Jones. It's 1966, and Jones has returned home after a stint in the press office in the Army in Vietnam. Over the course of the week captured in the novel, he gathers street stories, tall tales, rapturous sermons, reportage, artworks, mythologies, and family history into a vibrant commingling of a variety of experiences, told in a variety of registers — the bar itself is filled with "regular customers, opinionated drivers, blowsy fools, conmen supreme, saintly locals." The temporal restriction, combined with the wildness of its telling, suggest that Gates would've been closer to the truth had he called it the *Ulysses* of the African-American novel, as scholar John G. Cawelti did in his definitive review in *Callaloo*. But Forrest would have rejected the second part of the sentence. As he told one interviewer, "I was out to write the great American novel. Not the great *black* American novel." And, as Joubert says of his ambition to write the Great American Play, he wants "not to satisfy whites, but to live up to the enormous ambitions of the American Dream, spun within my soul by a family of Negroes who were as confused over what it meant to be an American as was Mister Lincoln."

Joubert is an echo of Forrest, who worked at a family-owned bar and liquor store, and served as a public information officer in the Army in the early 1960s. And just as Joubert gathers up the stories he hears from those around him, Forrest started his writing career as a reporter for *Muhammad Speaks*, the newspaper published by the Nation of Islam in Chicago. (His appreciation of the NOI was always muted, though, and it's a target for mockery in *Divine Days*.) Forrest had a keen understanding of the effect of race and racism on the Midwest from Reconstruction on down, and he funnelled that understanding into three linked novels that serve as supporting texts to *Divine Days*. *There Is a Tree More Ancient Than Eden* (1973), *The Bloodworth Orphans* (1977), and *Two Wings to Veil My Face*

(1983) all deal with the intersection of Forest County (modeled after Chicago's Cook County) and the violent, incestuous, and abusive pasts of its residents back in rural Mississippi.

Divine Days's mid-1960s setting allows Forrest to address the Southern roots of the Great Migration to Chicago alongside the rising tide of black protest during the Vietnam War—moments that Forrest perceived as moments of fracture and dispersal. That idea is embedded in the story's main secondary characters: Sugar-Groove, a South Side hipster, bon vivant, and story-spinner who's gone missing, and W.A.D. Ford, a corrupt storefront preacher at the church of the novel's title. Sugar-Groove is an inveterate storyteller about the history of African-Americans in the county, particularly their roots among New Orleans creoles. Sugar-Groove came North "to escape the aggravation," and the chief aggravation is race. The story returns often to the theme of his status as the son of a white landowner and his black mistress, who died in childbirth. Sugar-Groove's half-sister is killed by his brother, and he's headed north to escape death himself. Two lines reverberate, fugue-like, through the novel to highlight the sense of loss and betrayal Sugar-Groove's life represents. One is a ghostly utterance from his late mother, delivered to her master: "How could you destroy what we created?" The second is the chorus of Nat King Cole's hit "Nature Boy": "The greatest thing you'll ever learn / Is to love and to be loved in return." The former evokes the constancy of violence; the second, the impossible dream of transcending it.

Chicago is sanctuary—or, at least the suggestion of the possibility of one, of avoiding the legacy of Southern racism. "You can't look upon people from a standpoint of race, not in the long run, and be clearheaded and not get mad—and maybe even not go mad," Sugar-Groove says. "Because there aren't really any races, when all is said. There are only people, stocks, and cultures .... Now the memory text of the old was blown down the corridors of yesteryear. To survive they had to quickly readjust to the constant patter of overwhelming upheaval in the living present, or die out."

Instead of "legacy," love; instead of race, community. Joubert takes on listening to these stories — particularly a climactic battle in the desert between Sugar-Groove and Ford—as his Joycean duty, to take the city's stories and spin a mythology out of it." I was as thirsty for stories as those ghosts Ulysses meets are famished for the blood in the trenches, in order to achieve the power of speech. How else to stock my soul upon the lies and stories out of the mouths of others in order build up a stockpile of voices—beside the ones I continually heard—in order to become a playwright of a thousand voices?"

I wish *Divine Days* were broken up into chapters in Dickensian style, summarizing the preposterous events of each section. The book is best read in the same way you might read a Bulfinch's mythology, or a Bible—dipped into to extract a story, a riff, a sermon, an ode. Here, a tall tale about a man so heavy that his fall in Aunt Eloise's Night Light Lounge is tantamount to an earthquake. There, a variation on the tale of Moses in the bulrushes, this time with an abandoned baby discovered in an alley. Elsewhere, a conflagration between a police officer and a Nation of Islam representative over the morality of shooting a drug addict, or a story about a drug dealer's obsession with African masks. Every one of them is awash in humor, allegory, and willful digression. As Crouch memorably put it, *Divine Days* "reads the way a whale eats." But not all all-consuming books are so rooted in a particular place's sensibility the way *Divine Days* is. The novel rarely visits a section of Chicago outside the parcel of the South Side where Joubert Jones travels. But the point is that Chicago—and exclusively Chicago—is the kind of place that can take in this kind of multitude, both as the hub of the Great Migration and as the hub for the kind of storytelling that Joubert prizes. Forrest, like Joubert, is skeptical about anything resembling healing, but Forest County is an escape hatch from family tragedies of Mississippi and New Orleans.

Forrest made that point in an interview in 1995, two years before his death:

> Chicago is the city that captures this kind of rowdy spirit that, it seems to me, has been missing so much from African American letters. This blend of the sacred and the profane seems to me to be so much a part of the Northern experience, particularly a city like Chicago with its great possibilities of going for broke. It's a hustler's town. You can make a comeback after falling, and people will let you up. It's not bound up by class differences in the black community the way other cities are. The idea of open-ended possibility in Chicago of the black community is really, to some degree, true of the muscularity of Chicago in a general way; in other literatures, it's mellow. Because of that, my fiction seems to me to be set uniquely in a kind of Chicago, though I always call it Forest County work. The specific things—barbershops, bars, and churches—you can find those anyplace, but I hope they would have a certain Chicago character to them.

Religious but profane, hustling yet community-minded, informed by the past but eager to be free of class, muscular but compassionate. In Midwestern literature above all, this breadth of contradictions serve as a retort—proofs that the region hasn't locked into a set form, has never locked into a set form, pushes back, experiments, defies expectations. In *Divine Days*, a wild, violent, risk-taking novel whose heft demands you take it seriously and whose pages reward the effort, the contemporary Midwestern novel has a peculiar, reckless, and commanding classic.

"WHAT ABOUT...?"

A s I wrote in the introduction, this book is not intended to be a comprehensive study of contemporary Midwestern literature. That said, the urge to be as comprehensive as possible in a limited space is strong. While writing this book, I was often thinking of authors who couldn't be easily slotted into the broad categories of the book proper, or who are interestingly sui generis, or who have enough fans as quintessential contemporary Midwestern authors that it'd seem like bad form to ignore them. To that end, a few observations, recommendations, quips, and perhaps unfair dismissals.

Nelson Algren. For many, Algren is *the* definitive Chicago writer. I felt that way for a long time, too—his story collection *The Neon Wilderness* (1947) and prose poem *Chicago: City on the Make* (1951) are much-admired sketches of the city that he memorably likened to a pretty girl with a broken nose. And I still admire the latter for blending hard-edged yet lyrical perceptions of the city that are much imitated but unsurpassed. (Studs Terkel and Alex Kotlowitz have both tried their hand at *Make*-ish appreciations.) But the story pretty much stops there for me with Algren—his novels, including his 1949 National Book Award-winning *The Man With* *the Golden Arm,* are often clunky, with little to recommend them beyond an archival whiff of postwar Chicago.

Charles Baxter. Baxter is a native Minneapolitan and University of Minnesota professor who hasn't ignored his home turf. His 2003 novel, *Saul and Patsy,* follows a couple in Michigan ("this place smack out in the middle of nowhere") and an act of violence that undoes its bland comforts. But I tend of think of Baxter as a placeless writer, a critic who enjoys tinkering with fictional structures while keeping his backdrops determinedly unassuming. So the more playful Baxter is, the better he is, regardless of setting—I love his story "The Old Murderer" (in his 2012 collection, *Gryphon*) about the relationship between an alcoholic and a paroled felon who claims to be building a spaceship in his basement. His 2015 collection *There's Something I Want You to Do* features fictional sketches circling on the themes of vice and virtue, with a few hallucinatory scenes set in Minneapolis.

Willa Cather. Cather's Great Plains novels, *O Pioneers* (1913) and *My Ántonia* (1918), braid maternal themes with the notion of Manifest Destiny—her landscapes are fertility symbols for stories that turn on motherhood and end in marriage. But the remarkable novel she wrote between is a thematic counterweight: *The Song of the Lark* (1915) stars a woman, Thea, who's bristling with ambition, fervor, and attitude. Her father is skeptical of her dreams of going to Chicago to become an opera singer—he "believed that big cities were places where people went to lose their identity and to be wicked." Wicked? Nah. Lose your identity? Well, that's not the worst thing for a woman eager to break with convention. Here, the city's emotional blankness ("she had got almost nothing that went into her subconscious self and took root there") is a springboard.

Sandra Cisneros. Cisneros's breakthrough novel, 1991's *The House on Mango Street*, is a kind of cousin to Dybek's *The Coast of Chicago*, though the family she describes lacks the neighborhood stability his heroes do. Its narrator, a girl named Esperanza, has a modest version of the American dream ("our house would have running water and pipes that worked") that's complicated by crime and racial tensions ("watch us drive into a neighborhood of another color and our knees go shakity-shake"). The Loop is a fantasy: "you always get to look beautiful and get to wear nice clothes and can meet someone in the subway who might marry you." There and in her 2002 novel, *Caramelo*, which follows one family's travels between Chicago and Mexico City, she identified herself as one of the region's most prominent novelists of both race and class mobility. A follow-up would be welcome.

Louise Erdrich. Erdrich is the best-known Native American writer of the Midwest—and the fact that most critics would be hard-pressed to name the second-best-known points to her unique place in the regional literary firmament. Her Dakota-set stories evoke the flat, wind-blown landscape—much of her writing takes place in and around a small town called Pluto—but her turf is really the blurry line between Ojibwe and white traditions. That's laid out explicitly in her National Book Award-winning 2012 novel, *The Round House,* which turns on the question of who has jurisdiction over the rape of a Native American woman, and expanded in 2016's *LaRose*, which turns on a Native American family's obligation to one another and its community after an accidental murder.

Roxane Gay. Gay's 2014 novel, *An Untamed State*, reconceives the captivity novel for modern-day Haiti and the Midwest, and if those seem like two very different places, well, one of Gay's goals is to complicate the way we think about "exotic" and "conventional." Its heroine, Mirielle, has been kidnapped while visiting her native

Haiti and held for two weeks. She is repeatedly sexually assaulted there, despite the best efforts of her husband, Michael, to have her released. Mirielle is black, the daughter of a well-off family, and Michael is a white farm-boy from central Nebraska whose well-scrubbed demeanor impresses her parents. ("They call him Mr. America," as Mirielle puts it.) But America isn't exactly a safe alternative. After her escape, a PTSD-ish Mirielle acts out by heading to a bar where she banters with a man named Shannon who works in a local slaughterhouse, and the flirtation turns brutal in a way that mirrors his gig. ("He said I was Prime Grade.") A brutal dismissal of "Midwestern nice."

Jim Harrison. Intrigued by a former colleague's recommendation, I took a chance on Harrison's 1990 novella collection, *The Woman Lit by Fireflies*. Harrison is often compared to Hemingway, another Michiganer, but for me he mainly evokes his longtime friend Thomas McGuane, who wrote reams of gunky and dated troubled-guy fiction early in his career. A superb 2011 *Outside* profile by Tom Bissell, available online and in his fine collection *Magic Hours*, argues for Harrison as the last lion of two-fisted, whiskey-soaked fiction. I'm content to take Bissell's word for it.

Denis Johnson. Not a Midwestern author, despite a stint at the Iowa Writers' Workshop. But his descriptions of Chicago in his first novel, *Angels* (1983), are a beautiful and poignant portrait of hard-luck souls, particularly Jamie, who's bringing her baby girl on an ill-advised cross-country trip: "Clark Street at nine PM was a movie: five billion weirdos walking this way and that not looking at each other, and every third one had something for sale.... Jamie was struck with the peculiar notion that this scene of downtown Chicago was the projection of her daughter's infant mind."

Adam Langer. A longtime Chicago book and theater critic, Langer has written a pair of lively, bulky comic novels that revisit Chicago in the late 1970s and early 1980s—*Crossing California* (2001) and *The Washington Story* (2005). Between his efforts to out-Bellow Bellow and cover every middle-class waterfront in terms of race and religious identity (though North Side Jews in particular), both books can feel at once audaciously overwhelming and precious. But they're also consistently funny, and romanticize an era of the Midwest that's often neglected in favor of the gangster era and early postwar years.

Elmore Leonard. There may be no stronger argument for the cultural aversion to seeing Midwest fiction as an urban space than the fact that while Leonard set a third of his crime novels in his hometown of Detroit, none of them sourced the major TV and film adaptations (*Get Shorty, Jackie Brown, Out of Sight, Justified*) that made him a household name. But in 2014, Leonard was installed into the canon via the Library of America with a two-volume set mostly made up of his early Detroit-set novels like *Fifty-Two Pickup* (1974), which captured his vision of Detroit as a city grimed up by race riots and beginning its decline. He was lifelong a romantic for the place, but setting always took a back seat to the fast-moving crime story he was telling, and his romanticism was always blunt: "It was cool, about 40 degrees out, damp and overcast with a shitty-looking sky—spring in Detroit."

David Levine. A former U.S. Poet Laureate and Pulitzer winner, Levine was nostalgic for Detroit even before it was a place to be nostalgic about. His sinewy poems merged Whitmanesque celebrations of nature and the body with plainspoken rhetoric about life on the assembly line. In his 1999 poem "Belle Isle, 1949," he writes, "We stripped in the first warm spring night / and ran down into the Detroit River / to baptize ourselves in the brine of car parts, dead fish, stolen bicycles, / melted snow."

Michael Martone. A quintessential small-press experimentalist, Martone has produced a string of short novels that satirize his native state of Indiana and its products. The joke of *Pensees: The Thoughts of Dan Quayle* (1994) is that its subject is too dull to think; the joke of *The Blue State Guide to Indiana* (2001) is that the state barely qualifies for a travel guide in the first place. Yet Martone isn't so much down on the Hoosier State as he's eager to scrape off the homespun verities that have clung to it. In this Indiana, real wars get fought over Daylight Savings Time, Bill Blass's birthplace is a major attraction, Eli Lilly sponsors an amusement park, and a chapter on sports attractions includes no mention of basketball.

David Means. After more than three decades as an admired short-story writer tracking isolated types in Michigan, Means produced *Hystopia* (2016), a novel that proposed an alternative 1960s history in which Kennedy dodged a bullet in Dealey Plaza, the Vietnam War brought more even bad vibes stateside, and vets imperfectly tried to repress their memories via a drug called Tripizoid. From Michigan to Flint, Means's version of the state was one suffused with riots and fire, and one where a menacing Stooges song was always on whenever you were near a radio—a potent symbol for our collective Iraq/Afghanistan hangover.

Lorrie Moore. As a longtime creative writing professor at the University of Wisconsin–Madison, Moore was a Midwestern writer with plenty of influence on Midwestern writers. Ostensibly. But though her 2009 novel, *A Gate at the Stairs*, is set in a college town dubbed the "Athens of the Midwest," place has never been as meaningful to Moore as the spiky, darkly comic domestic conflicts she creates; "How to Become a Writer" is about how (not) to become a writer anywhere. In 2013, Moore left UW for Vanderbilt, prompting one resident to complain to the local alt-weekly about her relative invisibility in Madison, both in her writing and her physical presence. "Good riddance, Lorrie Moore," closed the correspondent.

Joyce Carol Oates. Oates won the National Book Award in 1970 for her 1969 novel, *them*, which centered on 1960s riots in Detroit; in 1974 she founded the *Ontario Review* just on the other side of the Detroit River. *Them* is an outlier in 1960s American fiction, a protest of protest novels. As Oates said in her acceptance speech, she was speaking out against "certain obsessions of mid-century Americans: a confusion of love and money, of the categories of public and private experience, of a demonic urge I sense all around me, an urge to violence as the answer to all problems, an urge to self-annihilation, suicide, the ultimate experience, and the ultimate surrender."

Stewart O'Nan. O'Nan's career achieved liftoff with 1999's Wisconsin-set *A Prayer for the Dying* (see "Somehow Form a Family"). And though he's rambled far from his native Pittsburgh in his fiction, from Boston to Niagara Falls to Jerusalem, the Midwest is never far from his vision: 2015's *West of Sunset* contemplates F. Scott Fitzgerald's last days in Hollywood through the filter of the uncertain St. Paul boy who made good. And one of his best novels, 2011's *Emily, Alone*, is rich with portraiture of Pittsburgh's transformation over the decades, focused as it is on the perspective on an elderly-but-hale heroine—a rare creature in contemporary fiction.

Harvey Pekar. Cleveland's modern poet of anxiety and self-loathing, Pekar created the long-running comic *American Splendor*, filled with his often-infuriated riffs on being unappreciated by editors, women, neighbors, "Old Jewish Ladies in Supermarket Lines," and, well, pretty much everyone. But for all his rage, a generosity of spirit shines through his vignettes—true crankcases don't get invited onto Letterman repeatedly and have films made of their life story. His chosen artists, especially Gerry Shamray, gave his Cleveland a no-nonsense, unabstracted feel that was perfect for his blunt, screw-you perspective. Pekar's beef was with the culture of everything's-great that surrounded him; he didn't mind taking the bus so much as the fact that the bus had a sign with the persistent 1970s local slogan, "The Best Things in Life Are Right Here in Cleveland."

Jayne Anne Phillips. Phillips has been obsessed with the mass murder of a family in her native West Virginia in 1930, the source material for her 2014 novel, *Quiet Dell*. But though the deed was done in Appalachia, the ill-fated family was from the Chicago suburbs, and the novel imagines the Midwest as rapidly transitioning from gullibility (the matriarch of the murdered Eichner clan believed the killer's guff about love and marriage) to streetwise female empowerment. (The lead *Chicago Tribune* reporter is a woman forced to prove herself on the job.)

Donald Ray Pollock. A longtime Ohio paper-mill worker who began a writing career in his 50s, Pollock uses his fiction to argue that his native southern Ohio is such a peculiar confluence of Midwestern (polite, agricultural), Southern (racist, churchy), and Appalachian (sawed-off) values that it's bound to be a powerkeg. His debut, *Knockemstiff* (2008) features a contemporary cast of pugnacious characters, but in his two novels (*The Devil All the Time* (2011); *The Heavenly Table* (2016)) he suggests that the problem stretches deep into the past century, where serial killers, soldiers, outlaws, and (especially) hyperreligious parental figures are determined to ruin the lives of those around them.

Richard Powers. If you were running a lab designed to produce a Brilliant Contemporary Midwest Author, you'd likely extrude something resembling Powers. Deep sense of history? Check. From his debut, *Three Farmers on Their Way to a Dance* (1985), in part a study of Henry Ford at the advent of World War I, to 2014's *Orfeo*, which reimagines the once-vibrant experimental music scene in central Illinois, he grasps the region's industrial and creative past. Smart on regional class and economics? *Gain* (1998), about a soap factory's rise to a carcinogenic chemical conglomerate, is as good as business novels get. Alert to the lay of the land? *The Echo Maker* (2006) parallels the fate of Nebraska's Platte River with the fate of a man's neurological injury. Which is to say that he writes more about intellect than place, and from a contemplative remove. His novels are always admirably smart but rarely visceral.

Veronica Roth. Roth's dystopian YA trilogy — *Divergent* (2011), *Insurgent* (2012), and *Allegiant* (2013) — imagines a shattered and tribal society fighting à la *The Hunger Games* in a future Chicago. I have a pet theory that dystopian novels are class novels by other means — ways to explore the ways that social institutions stratify our existences while dispensing with the drudgery of grown-up social-realist bricks. My only fear is that reading any further than I have in Roth's oeuvre will make such distinctions punishingly obvious. In *Divergent*, only elites get to ride the L train — elevated indeed.

Jean Thompson. With the marketplace doing everything it can to kill the midlist author, Jean Thompson's persistence is a remarkable achievement to be grateful for — she's among the most underrated fiction writers in the Midwest. *The Year We Left Home* (2011), tracks a family's fortunes in Iowa and Illinois with a Franzen-like sophistication; *She Poured Out Her Heart* (2016) cannily follows two female college friends and their divergent career paths in Chicago.

She's at her most inventive in 2014's *The Witch and Other Tales Retold*, a story collection that transplants fairy-tale characters into middle-lower-class Midwestern settings. Her Cinderella wears stripper heels.

Kurt Vonnegut, Jr. There's plenty of pride-of-place for Vonnegut in his native Indianapolis, which houses the library and museum dedicated to his work. But he always held the Midwest at arm's length in his fiction, which would sooner head off to other planets or the Galapagos Islands. The sole novel of his set in Indiana is 1965's *God Bless You, Mr. Rosewater*, and then not with much detail. That said, he's played an important role in defining the tone of contemporary Midwestern writing, which you might call Modified Twain—alternating between comic and sagely, but always unapologetically plainspoken. In Indianapolis, he once wrote, "common speech sounds like a band saw cutting galvanized tin, and employs a vocabulary as unornamental as a monkey wrench."

Acknowledgments

This book was inspired in part by "Reading the Midwest," a column I've written for *Belt Magazine* about Midwestern writers since 2014. I am deeply grateful to Anne Trubek for offering me the opportunity to write the column in the first place, and for her confidence that I could expand on it in these pages. Thanks also to Belt staffers Martha Bayne and Nicole Boose for helping to get this book out into the world.

I'm lucky to have many friends and colleagues who, when you tell them you're writing a book about Midwestern fiction, are eager to share their thoughts, suggestions, and support. So, many thanks to Janice Harayda, Laurie Hertzel, Meredith Hindley, Matthew Hunte, Anne Elizabeth Moore, Walton Muyumba, Bill Savage, Elizabeth Tamny, Elizabeth Taylor, Bill Tipper, and Ted Weinstein. Special thanks to Tina Casagrand and Kim Kankiewicz, who helped steer my thinking about the intersection of Midwestern history and literature, and about how slippery a word "Midwest" can be.

I live in Arizona now, but I'm a Midwesterner at heart: My parents came to Chicago from Greece and taught me much of what I know about place, assimilation, and the power of words. In addition to being a fellow classmate at Morton West High School in Berwyn, Illinois, Shawn Neidorf has been my dearest companion, best editor, and constant inspiration. We've moved around a lot together, but wherever she is, I'm home.

About the Author

Mark Athitakis has written on books for many publications, including the *New York Times, Washington Post, Minneapolis Star-Tribune, Barnes and Noble Review,* and *Belt Magazine,* which publishes his "Reading the Midwest" column. He lives in Arizona.